The GOURMET FARMER

deli book

The
GOURMET
FARMER

deli book

food as it used to taste

MATTHEW EVANS
NICK HADDOW
ROSS O'MEARA

CONTENTS

INTRODUCTION

This book is an ode to the old ways. It's a celebration of the way things should taste and used to taste. It rejoices in the old-fashioned, not for the sake of it, but for the taste of it. Because in so many ways the modern industrial food system has improved efficiency, yield and turnover times at the expense of flavour.

The three of us have been very blessed in life. We have been to the source of produce. Two of us run our own farms, the other a boutique cheesery. We have all fished in pristine waters, nurtured meals from the soil, even worked in quality restaurants. And now, in our little piece of paradise in southern Tasmania, we're preserving our own meat, firing up smokers, bottling fish and living a life many think only exists in Provence or Tuscany. The thing is, what makes our eating so good is at the fingertips of anybody who cares to give it a go.

Make your own Toulouse sausages and you'll be amazed at the difference. Smoke your own pork middles to discover the 'Lost Taste of Bacon'. Pot-set your own yoghurt, churn your own butter, brine your own olives and you'll not only be mesmerised by the distinction between yours and commercial products, but you will also discover that all too often the shortcuts used by the food industry are there for one thing only; profit. We, however, are focused on how the thing 'eats' when you carry out that most personal of acts; putting it in your mouth, chewing and swallowing. It's food produced without a manufacturer in mind — food that's aimed firmly at the cook and the eater.

We hope this celebration of old-fashioned methods opens up a whole new, boundless world where the variations possible are only limited by your time and imagination. Where the ham you make one day will taste not only different from anything you can buy, but a little different from the next ham you'll make, or the one after that. It's a book about putting your personal stamp on the tucker in your pantry and larder. We hope you enjoy delving into its depths as much as we enjoyed discovering the old, handcrafted ways too.

Matthew, Nick and Ross

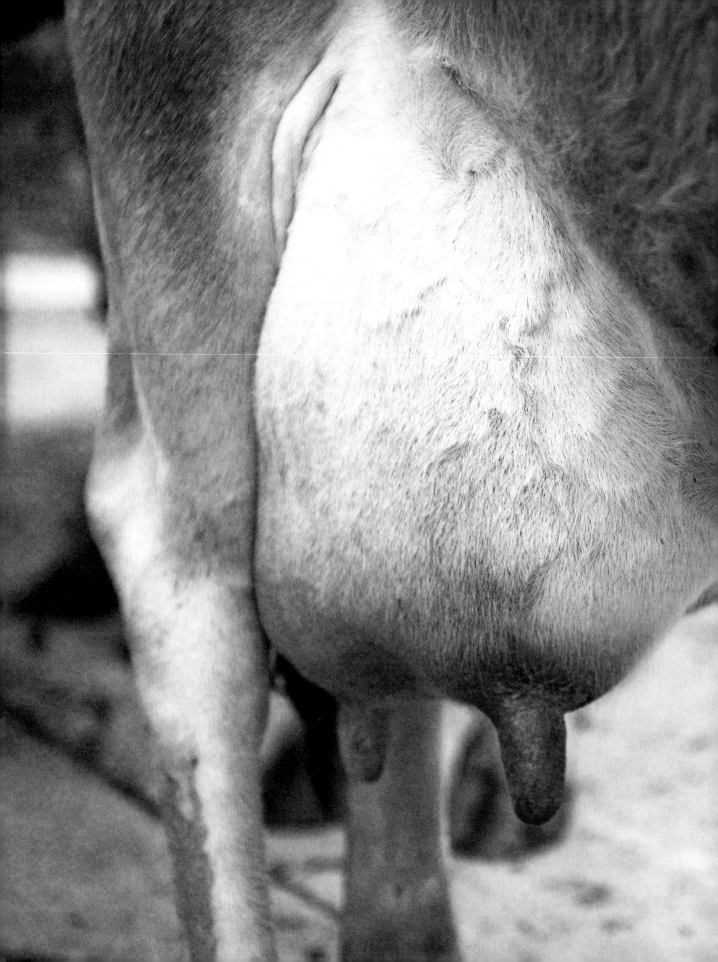

MILK

MILK

THERE ARE HUNDREDS OF REASONS NOT TO GO TO THE EFFORT OF MAKING YOUR OWN CHEESE, BUTTER OR YOGHURT AND ONLY ONE COMPELLING ARGUMENT TO DO IT: FLAVOUR.

Nowhere in the world of food has anything strayed so far off track as dairy products. A combination of excessive regulation, demands by supermarkets leading to mass production and the dumbing down of consumers has left us with shopping trolleys full of sickly sweet yoghurt, cream thickened with gums, butter with no flavour, cheese that never ripens and ricotta made from milk powder. How on Earth did we let this happen?

It can be startling how good homemade dairy produce can be when the true flavour of the milk is allowed to take centre stage. Sourcing good milk to start with is essential. It seems wrong to go to the trouble of making your own cheese or yoghurt from bog-standard supermarket milk. If you can't befriend a local dairy farmer to access your milk (remember, there are loads of smallholders who have a house cow or goat), then buy unhomogenised milk, ideally from one farm. We are lucky in Australia that there are more and more options available for sourcing this kind of milk.

Many of the processes in this chapter are quite simple, and really only just involve steering what happens if you let nature take its course. Hygiene is of paramount importance when making fresh dairy products, as most of the time what you are trying to do is create a perfect environment for good bacteria. Because the bad bugs are equally happy breeding in these conditions, you need to take steps to try and keep them out. Before making any of the recipes, make sure you wash, sterilise (using boiling water or chemicals, see page 4) and dry all of your equipment and your work space.

STERILISING BOTTLES

For all preserving you need to have your bottles, jars and other equipment free of bacteria or moulds or anything that could prove harmful if allowed to stay in the jar and affect the food. All jars and lids should be spanking clean AND sterile.

A dishwasher will not only clean the jars and lids, but the heat of the water will sterilise them. If you're hand washing jars, or using jars that have been stored for a while, you'll need to sterilise them using boiling water or a hot oven. Many people take the clean jars and place in cold water then bring to the boil. (The risk of jars shattering comes when there is a great change in temperature; hence the cool jars in cool water to start.) The difficult thing is removing the hot jars from the water and keeping them sterile without dropping them, though you can buy special tongs for this purpose.

Clean jars can also be put into a cool oven and heated to 100°C (200°F). You need to be careful when you heat the lids because if you heat them much past 100°C the rubber seals can melt or harden. The simplest sterilising method is the microwave; you can kill bacteria and spores by placing empty, clean and dry jars in the microwave for about 30 seconds per jar. However, this won't work for metal lids.

There are commercially available chemical sterilisers, often called sanitisers, which kill bugs too, and these are useful for sterilising lids, as well as the tools used for making salami or cheese. They're often found in the baby section of supermarkets. We try to avoid chemicals, so tend to use a big pot of boiling water to sterilise most utensils, and a mix of dishwasher and boiling water for sterilising jars and their lids. Remember, when you go to fill the jars, the heat of the jar should be about the same as the heat of the ingredient; so hot liquids should go into hot jars, cold liquids into cold (again, to avoid the risk of the glass shattering).

CREAM AND BUTTER

Okay, let's be honest — who thinks importing butter from France or Denmark is taking things a step too far? Sure, it might be justified when you consider that so much of the locally made commercial stuff is, at best, greasy and bland, and at worst, old and rancid, but come on! Luckily, there are a bunch of rogue butter makers in Australia now who are selling products that outshine top-shelf imported butter.

Australian butter should taste better, too. European butter is pale in comparison because it comes from cows that are largely grain-fed. Australian cows are almost exclusively raised on grass and the beta-carotene is passed into the milk and then the butter, giving it a yellow colour.

And while we are on a rant, have you looked at the ingredients label of your average supermarket cream lately? When did cream stop containing just cream and start needing gums, thickeners, sweeteners, acidity regulators and preservatives? The answer is, it doesn't. Supermarkets and huge manufacturers have led consumers down this path. We think it's now time to take a different path.

CLOTTED CREAM

Makes about 400 g (14 oz)

As far as old-fashioned comfort food goes, clotted cream is right up there with bangers and mash or a roast chook. It takes a bit of effort to make but it's well worth it. In essence, it is cream that has been very slowly baked, reducing the moisture content and allowing a caramelised crust to form on top. Make sure the cream you start with is pure cream with no thickeners — it works really well with 45% cream but this may be hard to get in some places. Serve clotted cream with berry jam on scones, dolloped on top of a pudding or straight from the end of your finger!

Allow the cream to sit at room temperature for 8 hours to slightly sour — this will greatly improve the taste of the clotted cream.

In a bowl, lightly whisk the cream. Pour into a 15 x 10 x 11 cm (6 x 4 x 4¼ inch) loaf (bar) tin so that the cream is 5.5 cm (2¼ inches) deep.

Preheat the oven to 100°C (200°F/Gas ½). Place the loaf tin into a larger baking dish or roasting tin and pour in enough water to come halfway up the sides of the dish. Bake the cream until it has reduced by up to a third and a golden crust has formed on top (this can take anywhere from 8 to 15 hours). Remove from the oven, allow to cool, then cover and refrigerate for 1–2 days to set.

Spoon the cream from the top and transfer to an airtight container, discarding any watery residue at the bottom of the tin. Clotted cream can be stored in the refrigerator for up to 1 week ... but we bet it doesn't hang around for that long!

700 ml (24 fl oz) thick pure cream (45%) — or use a combination of 350 ml (12 fl oz) pouring (whipping) cream (35% fat) and 350 ml (12 fl oz) double (thick/heavy) cream (52% fat)

CRÈME FRAÎCHE

Makes 500 g (1 lb 2 oz)

Crème fraîche is often considered to be a fancy way of saying sour cream but really they are quite different. Crème fraîche is cream that has been allowed to 'mature' under carefully controlled conditions. The natural bacteria in the cream is allowed to grow, converting the lactose in the cream to lactic acid, which 'thickens' the cream. Sour cream is a modern variation of this process and relies on the addition of bacteria to the fresh cream to achieve a similar result. This recipe will make a much softer textured crème fraîche than commercially made products, which usually include thickeners.

500 ml (17 fl oz/2 cups) pouring (whipping) cream (35%)

2 tablespoons cultured buttermilk (see note)

Make a double boiler using a large stainless steel bowl over a saucepan of simmering water. Pour the cream and buttermilk into the bowl and stir constantly until it reaches 25°C (77°F) — check using a kitchen thermometer.

Remove from the heat and immediately pour into sterilised glass jars (see page 4). Seal with tight-fitting lids, then place the jars into a large container, such as an esky or polysterene box with a lid. Pour in tepid (25°C/77°F) water so that it comes halfway up the sides of the jars. Cover the esky and leave for 12–36 hours, or until the cream appears thickened (don't shake the jars or the 'gel' will be destroyed).

Refrigerate the crème fraîche — it will continue to thicken and develop in flavour and can be stored this way for up to 2 weeks.

NOTE: *Real buttermilk is hard to find but if you make the cultured butter (see pages 12–13) you will have some 'live' cultured buttermilk. If not, substitute natural 'live' yoghurt (see pages 56–57) as your culture to begin the fermentation in the crème fraîche.*

CULTURED BUTTER

Makes about 400 g (14 oz) cultured butter
Yields about 400 ml (14 fl oz) buttermilk

Chances are you have already made butter accidentally by over-whipping cream and splitting it. Making butter really is that easy. Making cultured butter is not much harder but will give a great flavoured butter that makes the commercial stuff look like a block of insipid grease by comparison.

Pour the cream into a large sterilised glass jar (see page 4) and stir in the yoghurt. Seal with a tight-fitting lid and stand at room temperature, about 20°C (68°F), for 12–24 hours — the longer the time, the stronger the flavour will be.

Transfer the cream to the refrigerator and cool for a few hours.

Put the cream into the bowl of an electric mixer with a paddle attachment or use a butter churn if you have one. Process or churn on low speed — as the cream turns to butter it will first become whipped cream, then small granules of butter will appear. This is closely followed by buttermilk, which separates out while the butter granules become larger. When the butter and the buttermilk are separated, drain off and reserve the buttermilk (this should be retained for cooking or for use as a culturing agent to make more butter).   »

1 litre (35 fl oz/4 cups) pouring (whipping) cream (35%)

2 tablespoons natural 'live' yoghurt (pages 56–57) or cultured buttermilk (see method)

1 tablespoon pure fine sea salt or ½ teaspoon flaked sea salt (optional)

» Place 1 litre (35 fl oz/4 cups) chilled water into a sterilised glass jar and add the butter grains. Seal with a tight-fitting lid, then shake the jar for a few minutes — this helps to wash out the remaining buttermilk. If you want to make salted butter, you can add 1 tablespoon pure fine sea salt to the chilled water before shaking. (Alternatively, for salted butter with a nice crystalline crunch another option is to sprinkle in ½ teaspoon flaked sea salt when shaping the butter — see below). Drain and discard the liquid.

Transfer the washed butter to a clean chopping board. Use clean wet hands (or wooden butter pats if you have them) to gently work the butter grains together, kneading and squeezing out as much moisture as possible. You can divide it in half at this stage if it makes it easier to handle. Do this for about 5 minutes, then shape the butter and place in an airtight container. Store in the refrigerator for up to 2 weeks.

NOTE: *It is simple to clarify butter. Place 200 g (7 oz) butter in a small saucepan over low heat. Gently melt the butter and continue to heat until it begins to boil gently (the slower the better, otherwise you may burn the milk proteins). A layer of foam will appear on top and the milk solids will drop to the bottom — in between is the liquid clarified butter. Continue to boil gently until most of the foam disappears and the liquid on top becomes clear and golden. Carefully pour off the liquid into a bowl or jar — try not to let any of the solids in (these you can throw out). Place the clarified butter in the fridge and when it is solidified you can use it.*

FRANZ'S DAD'S CAFÉ DE PARIS BUTTER

Makes about 650 g (1 lb 7 oz)

Our friend, Franz Scheurer, has shared a brilliant recipe for this classic flavoured butter. It was originally created in 1941 by Freddy Dumont for the café of the same name, in Geneva, though the original recipe remains a secret. Franz's father's recipe dates from his time working at the Savoy in London in 1943. Yes, it does look like a scarily long list of ingredients, but they do all add their own nuances to the end product. It's worth making a bit of a batch as you can freeze it to use later. This butter transforms steak to something even more sublime, but is also terrific over spuds, beans or even under the skin of a roast chicken.

1½ tablespoons tomato sauce (ketchup) (page 242)

3 teaspoons dijon mustard

13 g (½ oz) capers (in brine), rinsed and squeezed dry

60 g (2¼ oz) French shallots, roughly chopped

1 small handful fresh curly parsley, chopped

2 tablespoons snipped fresh chives

1½ teaspoons dried marjoram

1½ teaspoons dried dill

1 teaspoon fresh thyme leaves

5 fresh French tarragon leaves

a pinch of ground dried rosemary

1 small garlic clove, squashed then very finely chopped

4 anchovy fillets, rinsed

2 teaspoons good brandy

2 teaspoons Madeira

½ teaspoon worcestershire sauce

¼ teaspoon sweet paprika

¼ teaspoon Keen's curry powder

a pinch of cayenne pepper

4 white peppercorns, crushed

zest of ¼ lemon

juice of ½ lemon

1 teaspoon finely grated orange zest

1 slightly heaped teaspoon salt

500 g (1 lb 2 oz) cultured butter (pages 12–13)

In a large non-reactive bowl, mix together all of the ingredients except the butter and leave to marinate in a warm part of the kitchen for 24 hours (a slight fermentation will occur).

The next day, transfer the mixture to a blender or food processer and blend to a purée, then push the mixture through a fine sieve.

Heat the butter in a saucepan over high heat until it just starts to foam, then remove from the heat and stir in the purée until well combined. Allow the butter to cool to room temperature, then cover it or store in an airtight container and refrigerate for several weeks. It's customary to cool the butter enough to be able to shape it into logs, then wrap the logs individually and cut off slices as you need them. The slices can be laid onto the top of a still-hot seared sirloin or similar and placed under the grill. The top of the butter starts to brown while the bit underneath is still cool enough to remain solid.

CREAM AND BUTTER

ROAST TOMATO AND CRÈME FRAÎCHE CUSTARD TART

Serves 6–8

The saying goes that real men do not eat quiche. Possibly that is true, but Real Food men can't get enough of it! When Nick worked at London's Neal's Yard Dairy, this was sold around the corner at Carluccio's Deli and it made the perfect lunch on the run. Be creative with what you add; chunks of smoked ham, smoked tuna or cold leftover sausages would be great. Or, if you are not a big meat eater, fresh asparagus or roast pumpkin work a treat.

SHORTCRUST PASTRY

340 g (11¾ oz) plain (all-purpose) flour

150 g (5½ oz) chilled butter, chopped

2–3 tablespoons iced water

FILLING

4 free-range eggs

1 free-range egg yolk

1 French shallot, peeled and finely chopped

400 g (14 oz) crème fraîche (page 9)

2 tablespoons chopped fresh flat-leaf (Italian) parsley

100 g (3½ oz/1 cup) grated gruyère cheese

300 g (10½ oz) preserved roast tomatoes (page 229), at room temperature and drained of excess oil

To make the shortcrust pastry, put the flour and butter into a food processor and pulse until the mixture resembles breadcrumbs. Gradually add the iced water, a little at a time, until the mixture starts to come together. Turn out onto a clean work surface and shape into a disc. Wrap in plastic wrap and refrigerate for 30 minutes.

Preheat the oven to 190°C (375°F/ Gas 5). Lightly grease a 25 cm (10 inch) round loose-based tart (flan) tin, about 3 cm (1¼ inches) deep.

Roll out the pastry on a lightly floured work surface to make a 3 mm (⅛ inch) thick circle large enough to line the base and side of the tin, leaving the excess to hang over the edge. Place on a baking tray and chill for 30 minutes.

Remove from the refrigerator, line the tart base with baking paper and weights and blind bake for 20 minutes.

Remove the weights and baking paper and return to the oven for a further 5 minutes, or until the base is golden. Before it cools, trim the pastry around the edges. Reduce the oven temperature to 160°C (315°F/Gas 2–3).

To make the filling, whisk together the eggs, egg yolk, shallots and crème fraîche in a bowl. Season with salt and freshly ground black pepper, then fold in the parsley and half of the cheese. Pour the mixture into the tart base, distributing the cheese evenly.

Bake in the oven for 20 minutes, then carefully remove from the oven (the tart is only half cooked at this stage). Top with the remaining cheese and the tomatoes. Return to the oven for a further 20 minutes, or until set. Serve warm or cool.

VEGETABLE BISTEEYA

Serves 12

This dish came about from Ross being married to a vegetarian. It is also great for a picnic. You will need a round pie tin or dish with a 25 cm (10 inch) diameter, about 5 cm (2 inches) deep, that you can heat from the bottom and also put in the oven. A Japanese cast-iron pan is perfect for this or you could use an ovenproof frying pan.

150 g (5½ oz) cultured butter (pages 12–13)

1 brown onion, thinly sliced

3 purple garlic cloves, crushed

1 bunch silverbeet (Swiss chard), washed and roughly chopped

1 bunch kale, washed and roughly chopped

1 bunch English spinach, washed and roughly chopped

1 bunch fresh flat-leaf (Italian) parsley, washed and roughly chopped

1 head broccoli, trimmed to small florets

1 tablespoon ground cumin

1 tablespoon ground coriander

1 teaspoon ground cinnamon, plus ½ teaspoon extra, for dusting

5 saffron threads, lightly toasted

150 g (5½ oz/about 7 sheets) fresh filo pastry

4 free-range eggs

100 g (3½ oz/1 cup) flaked almonds, toasted

1 tablespoon icing (confectioners') sugar

Heat half of the butter in a large heavy-based saucepan over medium heat. Add the onion and garlic and cook slowly for about 3 minutes. Add the silverbeet, kale, spinach, parsley and broccoli and cook until the greens start to break down. Once they have softened, add the cumin, coriander, cinnamon, saffron and 90 ml (3 fl oz) water and stir to combine. Reduce the heat to low, cover, and simmer for about 10 minutes. Strain the greens in a colander set over a bowl, reserving the cooking liquid.

Preheat the oven to 160°C (315°F/ Gas 2–3). Melt the remaining butter to use for the filo pastry. You must work quickly with filo so it doesn't dry out, keep any sheets you are not using under a damp tea towel (dish towel). Brush some butter in the base of a 25 cm (10 inch) round pie tin or dish, about 5 cm (2 inches) deep. Layer the filo in the base of the tin, brushing a little melted butter between each sheet and using about 7 sheets. Make sure as you place the pastry there is enough pastry to come back over the top to cover the pie. Cover with a damp tea towel and set aside.

Heat the reserved cooking liquid so that it is hot but not boiling. In a large bowl, beat the eggs to combine. Add the cooking liquid slowly to the eggs, stirring constantly. Add the greens and fold through.

Scatter a layer of almonds over the pastry at the bottom of the pie, then spoon in the filling mixture over the top. Fold the excess pastry over the pie to cover it completely.

Slowly heat the base of the pie tin over low heat to get some colour on the bottom (this will become the top later), being careful as the filo can burn very quickly — use a spatula to gently lift up one side to have a look and check.

Transfer to the oven and cook the bisteeya for 25–30 minutes, checking after 15 minutes. When the pie is set and golden, invert it gently onto a serving plate.

Combine the icing sugar and extra cinnamon and dust over the pie. Heat up a metal barbecue skewer and make criss-cross burn marks in a lattice fashion for decoration. Serve straight away.

BUTTER CAKE

Serves 8

There is nothing better, or simpler, than a warm butter cake with a mug of strong tea. Nick's mum used to make a cake similar to this, sprinkle some brown sugar and cinnamon over the top and serve it in slices that were spread with even more butter!

Preheat the oven to 180°C (350°F/Gas 4). Grease and line the base and side of a 22 cm (8½ inch) round cake tin with baking paper.

Using an electric mixer, cream together the butter, sugar and vanilla seeds on medium–high speed until light and fluffy. Add the eggs, one at a time, beating well after each addition until combined. Add half each of the flour and milk and stir to combine. Repeat with the remaining flour and milk, stirring until just combined.

Spread the mixture into the prepared tin, smoothing the top. Bake in the oven for 50–60 minutes, or until a skewer inserted into the centre of the cake comes out clean. Leave to cool in the tin for 10 minutes, before turning out onto a wire rack to cool completely. Cut into slices and serve.

250 g (9 oz) cultured butter (pages 12–13), softened

220 g (7¾ oz/1 cup) caster (superfine) sugar

1 vanilla bean, split lengthways and seeds scraped

3 free-range eggs

375 g (13 oz/2½ cups) self-raising flour, sifted

250 ml (9 fl oz/1 cup) full-cream (whole) milk

OPEN SANDWICH WITH PASTRAMI AND CRÈME FRAÎCHE

Makes 1

This is a great sandwich for any time of day — when you start using things you can make yourself it suddenly becomes a whole lot better.

PER SANDWICH

2 generous slices light rye bread, buttered

1 teaspoon Ross's wholegrain mustard (page 248)

roughly 1 tablespoon three-day pickled cabbage (page 226) or sauerkraut (page 227)

4 thin slices pastrami (page 107)

1 tablespoon crème fraîche (page 9)

Lay one piece of bread on a cutting board and smear with the mustard. Top with the cabbage and pastrami. Spread the other piece of bread generously with the crème fraîche and lay over the top. Cut in half and eat noisily and greedily.

CLOTTED CREAM FUDGE

Makes 36 pieces

Many British travel guides would have you believe that the streets of Cornwall are paved in clotted cream fudge, but in all of his travels to cheese farms in the region, Nick only ever saw the real stuff a couple of times. But no matter, it will be just as authentic when you use this recipe and make it at your place.

Place the sugar, golden syrup, clotted cream, whiskey and vanilla seeds into a small, deep heavy-based saucepan over low heat and stir until the sugar dissolves. Continue to cook over low heat until the mixture comes to the boil, cover the pan with a lid and boil for 3 minutes. Uncover and continue to boil until the temperature reaches 116°C (240°F) — you can use a kitchen thermometer to check this.

Remove from the heat and beat with a wooden spoon until most of the bubbles have subsided and the mixture starts to thicken slightly. Pour into a lightly greased shallow 15 cm (6 inch) square cake tin. Leave to cool to room temperature, then refrigerate until chilled. Invert the fudge, tapping the base and lifting off the tin. Cut the fudge into 2.5 cm (1 inch) squares to eat. Store in an airtight container in the refrigerator for up to 2 weeks.

NOTE: *If you can't find (or be bothered to make) clotted cream, a really thick cream (52%) will do a similar job, but without the 'caramel' flavour of clotted cream.*

275 g (9¾ oz/1¼ cups) caster (superfine) sugar

100 g (3½ oz) golden syrup

225 g (8 oz) clotted cream (page 8) or use store-bought clotted cream if you must

1 teaspoon whisky

1 vanilla bean, split lengthways and seeds scraped

FRESH CHEESES

We don't eat enough fresh cheese in Australia. Cheese, it seems, is something we only reach for at the end of the meal. Yet, the simple beauty of a delicate fromage blanc topped with a handful of ripe berries or a tangy goat's curd warmed on toast and finished with a pungent olive oil is undeniably satisfying.

Fresh cheeses do not have the benefit of maturation, rind development, moulds or bacteria to derive their flavour. Instead, they rely inherently on the quality of the milk. And their freshness. Ricotta, still warm from the making, is a revelation. Fromage blanc, barely set and smacking of lemony lactic acid, or a goaty, briny feta can redefine the simple beauty that is milk in all its forms.

Some of our most memorable moments eating cheese involve fresh cheese — curd which has only just been transformed but has captured all the delicate nuances of the milk; the breed of the animal, the flavour of the grass the animal has grazed upon ... even the air it has breathed are all recorded like a photograph and laid bare, free of any other influences.

FROMAGE BLANC

Makes about 1 kg (2 lb 4 oz)

Fresh, homemade cheese is easier to make than most people think and it tastes better than anything you can buy. Fresh cheese does not travel well and has a very short life due to its high moisture content. Fromage blanc is the purest expression of fresh cheese but it does rely on a good-quality milk for the bulk of its flavour, so start with unhomogenised milk, as fresh as you can get it. You are also going to need to find some rennet (see note, page 33). This fromage blanc has cream added to it. This is because a lot of people have asked us for a 'cream cheese' recipe. Adding cream gives a richer flavour and a more dense texture. You can make it with less or even no cream for a pure version but it's pretty good with a bit of cream.

Make a double boiler using a large stainless steel bowl over a large saucepan of simmering water. Pour the milk, cream and yoghurt into the bowl and stir constantly until it reaches 35°C (95°F) — check using a kitchen thermometer.

Remove the pan from the heat and place in a water bath of 35°C (use your sink with the plug in it) — use the thermometer to ensure the cream mixture is kept at a constant temperature.

In a separate non-reactive bowl, combine the rennet with 100 ml (3½ fl oz) cooled boiled water. Add this to the warm milk mixture and stir thoroughly for 3 minutes. Use your spoon to stop the milk from moving (you need it completely still while the rennet is working). Cover and leave for 1 hour, then check to make sure the curd is firm and set — it should come away from the sides of the bowl easily and you should be able to press your fingers on it gently without it breaking. Leave for longer if necessary.   »

1.5 litres (52 fl oz/6 cups) full-cream (whole) unhomogenised milk

1 litre (35 fl oz/4 cups) pouring (whipping) cream (35%)

250 g (9 oz/1 cup) natural 'live' yoghurt (pages 56–57) (see note)

rennet (consult the packet for dosage rates as these may vary between brands) (see note, page 33)

muslin (cheesecloth)

» Use a knife to cut the curd into 5 cm (2 inch) cubes — this will assist the whey to escape from the cut surfaces. Let it sit undisturbed for a further 15 minutes. Using a slotted spoon, very gently lift the curds into a colander or sieve lined with a few layers of muslin. Fold the excess cloth over the top and cover with plastic wrap. Place the colander in a bowl to catch the drips and refrigerate to drain the whey — the fromage blanc can be eaten, very soft (unsalted) after only 1 hour or will be firmer after about 8 hours.

After draining, transfer to a bowl, season with salt, to taste (omit salt if using in a sweet recipe), and stir well or you can gently whisk to remove any lumps. Store in an airtight container in the refrigerator for up to 3 days.

Lightly toast some of your favourite sourdough and spread it with drained fromage blanc. Eat it simply or finish it with a drizzle of good olive oil, season with salt and pepper and top with ripe tomato or avocado and some chopped parsley. You can even add a poached egg and sautéed spinach. Or, if you prefer something sweet, spread a spoonful of jam or honey over the top and enjoy.

NOTE: *We use natural 'live' cultured yoghurt to culture the milk. If you can't make your own (pages 56–57), look for any yoghurt that has 'live cultures' on the label. If you are going to make this regularly, or if you want to experiment, it would be worth getting some cheese cultures from online cheesemaking suppliers.*

FETA CHEESE

Makes about 800 g (1 lb 12 oz)

Yields about 4 litres (140 fl oz) whey

We are not really supposed to call it feta anymore, since the Greeks won the legal right to protect the name, but we reckon home cheesemakers are pretty safe from the lawyers. Fair enough too, the Greeks have been making feta for longer than almost any other cheese and what has been passed off under the name feta in recent times is shocking. Feta is a great place to start your home cheesemaking journey. It is a fairly simple process and the drained whey can be saved and used to make ricotta (see page 34).

Put the milk into a large saucepan over low heat, stirring regularly to prevent it from catching on the base of the pan, until it reaches 32°C (90°F) — check using a kitchen thermometer.

Half-fill the sink with warm water and sit the pot in it like a bain marie — this will stop the milk from cooling — it is important to maintain a constant temperature of 32°C for the entire process. Add the yoghurt and mix to combine, then allow to sit for 1 hour, still in the warm water bath, stirring occasionally.

In a non-reactive bowl, combine the rennet with 250 ml (9 fl oz/1 cup) of cooled boiled water. Add to the milk mixture and whisk vigorously for 3 seconds to combine. Use your spoon to stop the milk from moving (you need it completely still while the rennet is working). Cover and leave at room temperature, about 18–20°C (64–68°F) for 4–6 hours — do not disturb during this time. Check to make sure the curd is firm and set — it should come easily away from the side of the bowl.

Use a knife to cut the curd into 1 cm (½ inch) cubes. Do this by slicing the curd vertically in one direction, then again at right   »

5 litres (175 fl oz) fresh goat's milk (or use unhomogenised bottled goat's milk)

1 tablespoon natural 'live' yoghurt (pages 56–57)

rennet (consult the packet for dosage rates as these may vary between brands) (see note)

100 g (3½ oz) pure sea salt

1 tablespoon white vinegar

muslin (cheesecloth)

» angles — use a spoon to make the horizontal cuts as best you can — this can be a little tricky as the curd is quite soft and delicate at this stage.

Allow the curds to sit and 'rest' for 10 minutes, then gently stir the curds to stop them from knitting back together, stirring using a spoon every 5 minutes for the next 30 minutes. Line a colander or sieve with a few layers of muslin (cheesecloth), set over a bowl and drain the curds from the whey, reserving the whey (keep it refrigerated and use it to make the ricotta on page 34).

Find a plate big enough to cover the curds in the colander and act as a weight. Fold the excess muslin over the curds and place the plate on top. After 2–3 hours turn it over to help it drain evenly. Replace the plate and leave to drain for a further 6 hours or overnight.

To make a brine solution, in a large bowl mix together the salt, vinegar and 1.5 litres (52 fl oz/6 cups) water, stirring to dissolve the salt. Cut the drained cheese into large cubes (or into 1 cm/ ½ inch slices if making the baked feta recipe on page 43) and put in a large sterilised glass jar (see page 4). Pour over the brine solution to cover, then seal with a tight-fitting lid and let the feta 'pickle' in the refrigerator for a couple of days before eating. The feta will keep for up to 1 month in the brine and can be used in many different ways.

NOTE: *Rennet is a coagulant and is made from an enzyme — it is what turns the milk from a liquid into a solid. Rennet is available from home cheesemaking suppliers on the internet. There are a few different types, including traditional animal rennet and non-animal vegetarian rennet. Use them according to the directions from the supplier. If you can't get your hands on any rennet, some supermarkets still stock junket tablets. These are similar to rennet but sold in tablet form.*

RICOTTA AND PANEER

Makes 800 g (1 lb 12 oz) ricotta or 750 g (1 lb 10 oz) paneer

Making ricotta at home is as easy as falling off a log but the trick to making a true ricotta is to make it from whey, which means you first need to make some cheese to get the whey (see the recipe for feta, pages 32–33). If you use whey you will need to add 1 litre (35 fl oz/ 4 cups) full-cream (whole) milk to increase the yield. If you are not starting with whey, the good news is you can follow the same method using milk to make a paneer (see note).

Put the whey or milk into a large saucepan over low heat, stirring regularly to prevent it from catching on the base of the pan, until it reaches 60°C (140°F) — check using a kitchen thermometer. If you are using whey, add 1 litre (35 fl oz/4 cups) milk now.

Stir in the salt and continue to heat the mixture until it gets to 92°C (198°F) — do not let it boil or it denatures the protein and will prevent it from forming good curds. Remove from the heat and stir in the vinegar diluted with 200 ml (7 fl oz) water. Allow to rest for 1 minute — you will see the curds rise to the top.

Line a colander or sieve with a few layers of muslin and set over a bowl. Use a slotted spoon to lift the curds into the colander to drain the whey; allow to cool. Eat within a couple of days — keep refrigerated.

NOTE: *Paneer is not a real cheese — it is really just curdled milk which has been strained and hung. To make paneer, follow the method above using milk instead of whey — instead of draining the ricotta curds, bring the corners of the muslin together and tie into a bundle. Hang this over the sink or a bucket overnight at 18–20°C (64–68°F) or you can hang it in the refrigerator.*

4 litres (140 fl oz) whey (pages 32–33) for ricotta or full-cream (whole) unhomogenised milk for paneer

1 tablespoon salt

150 ml (5 fl oz) white vinegar

muslin (cheesecloth)

MASCARPONE

Makes 680 g (1 lb 8 oz)

Strictly speaking, mascarpone is not really a cheese because it has not undergone any fermentation. Draining the cream really concentrates its flavour and richness, making it the perfect partner for coffee or chocolate. A dash of rum, liqueur or a vanilla bean can make it even better. As always, the best quality cream will give the best results — buy one that has no thickeners.

1 litre (35 fl oz/4 cups) pouring (whipping) cream (35%)

1 tablespoon white vinegar

muslin (cheesecloth)

Make a double boiler using a large stainless steel bowl over a stockpot or large saucepan of simmering water. Pour the cream into the bowl and slowly bring to 90°C (194°F) — check using a kitchen thermometer. If you are going to add a vanilla bean, do it now.

Add the vinegar and stir constantly for a couple of minutes until the cream curdles slightly and begins to separate. Remove from the heat and allow to cool for about 15 minutes.

Line a colander or sieve with a couple of layers of muslin and sit the colander inside a bowl. Slowly pour the warm cream into the colander and refrigerate for 24 hours to allow the cream to drain and thicken. Discard the liquid in the bowl and transfer the mascarpone to an airtight container. Mascarpone can be stored in the refrigerator for up to 3 days.

FROMAGE BLANC CUPS WITH HONEY AND SPICED NUTS

Serves 6

This makes the most wonderful dessert and is a great way to enjoy the simple beauty of fresh fromage blanc. We served these at one of our A Common Ground luncheons to show off the milk from Matthew's jersey cow.

100 g (3½ oz/⅔ cup) almonds, chopped

100 g (3½ oz/⅔ cup) hazelnuts, chopped

50 g (1¾ oz) butter, softened

½ teaspoon mixed spice

200 g (7 oz) honey

500 g (1 lb 2 oz) unsalted fromage blanc (pages 30–31)

In a dry frying pan, cook the almonds and hazelnuts over medium heat until golden.

Add the butter, mixed spice and 1 tablespoon of the honey and continue to stir until well combined, about 3 minutes. Remove from the heat and set aside to cool.

Place a couple of generous spoonfuls of fromage blanc in the bottom of a serving cup or glass. Top with a spoonful of honey, then spoon the nut mixture over the top to serve.

WATERMELON, FETA AND MINT SALAD

Serves 4–6

While most of the time we find fruit in a salad just a healthy way to eat dessert, the salty sting of feta and a pungent cold pressed olive oil bring out a wonderful mouthwatering feel in this savoury salad. It's light, and when the melon is in season the flavours snap you to attention without overwhelming anything else in the meal.

It's just a tossed salad. Put the watermelon and feta in a bowl. The mint leaves should be shredded finely by stacking them up and cutting them crossways. Pop them in the bowl with the onion and give it all a bit of a toss.

Throw in the lime juice (sprinkle to distribute it well) with the olive oil and plenty of freshly ground black pepper. A great olive oil will make all the difference. We also like to add a few shreds of chilli sometimes, too. Mix it all up, and add a pinch or two of pure sea salt to bring out the flavours. Serve in the centre of the table with chargrilled barbecued meats.

¼ small ripe watermelon, seeded and cut into 2 cm (¾ inch) cubes

200 g (7 oz) feta cheese (pages 32–33), cut into 5 mm (¼ inch) cubes or crumbled

10 fresh mint leaves (or even better, a mix of mint and basil leaves)

1 small red onion, thinly sliced

1 tablespoon lime or lemon juice

60 ml (2 fl oz/¼ cup) extra virgin olive oil

BAKED FETA WITH PRESERVED TOMATO, OLIVES AND OREGANO

Serves 4

This is a bit of a Greek classic and is a great way to highlight your handiwork. It's a beautiful side dish for fish or chicken but bulk it up with a cup of chickpeas and some strips of roast capsicum if you need something more substantial.

2½ tablespoons extra virgin olive oil

500 g (1 lb 2 oz) feta cheese (pages 32–33), cut into 1 cm (½ inch) slices

1 red onion, sliced

60 g (2¼ oz/⅓ cup) black pickled olives (page 228)

180 g (6½ oz) preserved roast tomatoes (page 229), drained of excess oil

2–3 garlic cloves, crushed

4 fresh oregano sprigs

Preheat the oven to 160°C (315°F/Gas 2–3). Cut four large squares of foil and drizzle with the olive oil — these will be used to make four individual feta parcels.

Divide the feta slices between each piece of foil, then top with some of the onion, olives, preserved tomato, garlic and a sprig each of oregano. Fold the foil over the top to seal and enclose each parcel. Place on a baking tray and cook in the oven for 20 minutes, or until the feta is soft and slightly melted and the onion is cooked through. These feta parcels are good served as a starter or with bread and salad.

ROSS'S RICOTTA TART

Serves 8–10

*Ross kindly gave up his ricotta tart recipe. It's almost like a
shortcake mixture sandwiching lightly sweetened ricotta.*

To make the pastry, put the flour, sugar, icing sugar, baking powder, salt and butter into a food processor and pulse until the mixture resembles breadcrumbs. Add the eggs, and pulse to combine, then turn the mixture out onto a clean work surface and massage gently into a ball. Pull off one-third of the dough to use as the lid; the remainder will be the base. Roll into balls, cover in plastic wrap and refrigerate for 1 hour.

To make the ricotta filling, combine all of the ingredients in a large bowl. Set aside.

Preheat the oven to 180°C (350°F/Gas 4). Lightly grease a 26 cm (10½ inch) loose-based tart (flan) tin, about 3 cm (1¼ inches) deep.

Roll out two-thirds of the dough (the large ball) into a circle large enough to line the base and side of the tin, about 5 mm (¼ inch) thick. This dough is quite fragile so you need to work quickly — rolling the pastry out between sheets of baking paper is a good idea. If it is a hot day it may be necessary to transfer the pastry in the paper onto a large baking tray and firm it up in the refrigerator before lining the tin.

Gently press the ricotta filling evenly into the base and fold the pastry over the top a little. Roll out the remaining pastry into a circle large enough to fit the top, then lay it over the filling and pinch the edges together to seal, trimming any excess. Cook in the oven for 20–30 minutes, or until golden. Allow to cool in the tin before removing and serving at room temperature, dusted with extra icing sugar and the cinnamon, if desired.

PASTRY

300 g (10½ oz/2 cups) plain (all-purpose) flour

50 g (1¾ oz/¼ cup) caster (superfine) sugar

3 tablespoons icing (confectioners') sugar, sifted, plus extra, for dusting

1 tablespoon baking powder

a large pinch of pure sea salt

125 g (4½ oz) butter, chilled and diced

2 free-range eggs

ground cinnamon, for dusting (optional)

RICOTTA FILLING

650 g (1 lb 7 oz/2¾ cups) fresh ricotta (page 34)

3 free-range egg yolks (or use 2 whole eggs if you want)

3 tablespoons icing (confectioners') sugar, sifted

finely grated zest of 1 large lemon

SAAG PANEER

Serves 4

Ross and Nick are both married to vegetarians so this dish is a bit of a staple in their homes. Although it is a traditional Punjabi recipe, Nick and Ross both did time in the restaurant scene in London, the New World home of Indian food, where Ross perfected this recipe. Serve it with fresh roti or naan bread to mop up the sauce.

450 g (1 lb) English spinach leaves

2½ tablespoons clarified butter (see note, page 13) or vegetable oil

250 g (9 oz) paneer (page 34), cut into large cubes

1 onion, finely chopped

1 thumb-sized piece fresh ginger, peeled and finely chopped

4 tomatoes, chopped

1 teaspoon chilli powder

1 teaspoon ground coriander

¼ teaspoon ground turmeric

¼ teaspoon pure sea salt

3 teaspoons lemon juice

25 g (1 oz) unsalted butter

Put 600 ml (21 fl oz) water into a saucepan and bring to the boil. Blanch the spinach for 5 minutes, then drain well, reserving the cooking water. Mash the spinach or place in a food processor to make a purée and set aside.

Heat the clarified butter in a frying pan over medium heat. Add the paneer pieces and cook until light brown, turning to make sure they cook evenly on all sides. Remove from the pan and set aside.

In the same pan, cook the onion and ginger for 3–4 minutes. Add the tomato and sprinkle with the chilli, coriander, turmeric and salt. Cover and cook for 2–3 minutes, then add the spinach and stir through the lemon juice. If it is too dry, use about 2 tablespoons of the reserved spinach water to moisten the curry. Add the paneer to the pan. Remove from the heat and serve with the butter over the top.

SMOKED RICOTTA

Makes 800 g (1 lb 12 oz) ricotta

You need to use freshly made ricotta for this recipe. You can create endless dishes with it and the texture is amazing. We have a small electric smoker that works really well for this but you can use a wok with a lid and a wire rack. If you don't have a lid, a large wide bowl turned upside down over the top works just as well.

Lift the freshly made ricotta curds into a sieve lined with muslin as directed on page 34 and then press by topping with a plate and weight if needed. Leave in the refrigerator overnight to firm up.

First, put the wood chips in 2 tablespoons water and leave them to soak for 20 minutes.

Line the smoker or wok with a sheet of foil and place the wood chips on top.

Slowly heat the wood chips over low heat until they start to smoulder, then place a wire rack over the top and sit the ricotta on the rack. Cover with a lid and smoke for 15 minutes — this is about all you will need to get some of the smoke flavour into the cheese. If you want more smoke flavour, add more wet wood chips and smoke it for longer.

Serve warm from the smoker with a touch of olive oil or break it up into a delicious pasta.

1 quantity fresh ricotta (page 34)

1 cup of wood chips (preferably hardwood)

MASCARPONE AND TOASTED ALMOND SEMIFREDDO

Serves 8–10

250 ml (9 fl oz/1 cup) pouring (whipping) cream (35%)

120 g (4¼ oz/½ cup) mascarpone (page 35)

60 ml (2 fl oz/¼ cup) amaretto liqueur

2 free-range eggs, beaten

4 free-range egg yolks, beaten

110 g (3¾ oz/½ cup) caster (superfine) sugar

95 g (3¼ oz/¾ cup) slivered almonds, lightly toasted (see note)

Put the cream, mascarpone and amaretto in the bowl of an electric mixer with a whisk attachment, and whisk until the mixture begins to hold its shape but is still soft. Refrigerate until needed.

Put the egg, egg yolk and sugar in a stainless steel bowl over a saucepan of simmering water, making sure the base of the bowl does not touch the water. Whisk together until the mixture has increased in volume and thickens, about 5 minutes. Remove the bowl from the heat and continue whisking for a further 5 minutes, or until the mixture has cooled. Fold in 65 g (2¼ oz/½ cup) of the toasted almonds and the whipped cream.

Lightly grease and line the base and sides of a 1.25 litre (44 fl oz/5 cup) capacity rectangular mould with baking paper, leaving a 10 cm (4 inch) overhang on all sides. Pour the semifreddo mixture into the mould, cover with the excess baking paper and then with plastic wrap, and freeze for 12 hours or overnight.

Turn out the semifreddo from the mould and cut into slices. To serve, sprinkle the remaining almonds over the top.

NOTE: *To toast the slivered almonds, place them on a baking tray and put them in a preheated 150°C (300°F/Gas 2) oven for 10 minutes, or until golden, being careful as they will burn easily.*

FRESH CHEESES

51

TIPSY CAKE WITH ORANGE BLOSSOM MASCARPONE

Serves 3–4

Tipsy cake is also known as trifle. This recipe uses savoiardi (lady fingers) biscuits but isn't tiramisu (although it is equally as good).

In a bowl, mix together the mascarpone with 2 tablespoons of the icing sugar, the orange blossom water, orange zest, 2 tablespoons of the orange juice and the egg yolks.

In a separate bowl, whisk together the egg whites with 2 tablespoons of the icing sugar until soft peaks form. Fold one-quarter of these whites through the mascarpone mixture to lighten, then fold in the remaining whites, until just combined.

Whisk the remaining orange juice with the sherry and remaining icing sugar in a bowl until the icing sugar has dissolved. Soak each biscuit in this liquid, placing immediately in the bottom of a 1 litre (35 fl oz/4 cup) capacity serving bowl or individual serving dishes — use half the biscuits like this. Top with half of the mascarpone mixture, then repeat with the remaining soaked biscuits (mixing up more of the liquid if you run out) and finishing with the remaining mascarpone. Refrigerate for at least 3 hours before serving with the grated chocolate sprinkled on top.

- 250 g (9 oz/1 cup) mascarpone (page 35)
- 60 g (2¼ oz/½ cup) icing (confectioners') sugar, sifted
- 2 teaspoons orange blossom water (or try Grand Marnier)
- 1 teaspoon finely grated orange zest
- juice of 1 orange
- 2 free-range eggs, separated
- 125 ml (4 fl oz/½ cup) sweet sherry (or try brandy)
- 12 savoiardi (lady fingers) biscuits
- 50 g (1¾ oz) dark chocolate, grated

YOGHURT

What we get away with calling yoghurt these days is a disgrace. Sugar, preservatives, protein powder, thickeners, gums … it's almost impossible to find a commercially made yoghurt without any of these. It seems we have forgotten what real yoghurt is and how to make it. Compared to the bought stuff, homemade yoghurt is a revelation.

The basic principle in making yoghurt is that first you have to heat-treat the milk to kill any bad bacteria that might cause the yoghurt to spoil. Then, once this has been done, the highly active yoghurt bacteria have no competition so can quickly produce the lactic acid which gives good yoghurt its flavour and texture. Heating the milk also changes the nature of the protein and helps to thicken the yoghurt.

Milk is largely just protein (casein) in suspension and of all the milks available, cow's milk has the lowest protein so making yoghurt with sheep's or goat's milk will produce a thicker result. If you want to use cow's milk and don't want to strain it (see recipe, pages 56–57) you could add about 10 per cent milk powder to the volume of milk (say 100 g milk powder per 1 litre of milk) — this just boosts the protein content of the milk and makes the yoghurt more 'solid' but it also changes the ethos a bit too.

HALSEY SWETZOFF'S NATURAL YOGHURT

Makes 1.5 litres (52 fl oz/6 cups) natural 'live' yoghurt
or 900 g (2 lb) Greek-style yoghurt (after draining)

*Homemade muesli topped with thick 'live' yoghurt and fresh fruit may not be the
breakfast of champions, but on Bruny Island it is certainly the breakfast of cheesemakers.
This is a strained Greek-style yoghurt — straining increases the thickness of the yoghurt
and also the protein content. Halsey is an American cheesemaker who works at the
Bruny Island Cheese Co. This recipe, named after him, is one of the best we've tasted.
We make it using full-cream (whole) milk (this can be raw milk from a farmer or
unhomogenised milk from the shop) but it can also be made with skim milk.
To start the fermentation, use a few spoons of commercial 'live' yoghurt as the starter.*

Put the milk into a large saucepan over medium heat, stirring regularly to prevent it from catching on the base of the pan, until it reaches 80°C (176°F) — check using a kitchen thermometer.

Half-fill the sink with cold water and sit the pan in it, like a bain marie. Stir the milk until the temperature of the milk lowers to about 35°C (95°F).

Pour the warm milk into sterilised glass jars (see page 4) and evenly divide the yoghurt between the jars. Stir the contents of each jar for a couple of minutes to make sure the ingredients are well combined, then seal with tight-fitting lids.

Now you have to find something that will act as an incubator. Essentially you need to hold the temperature of the yoghurt at around 45°C (113°F) for 8–12 hours. This can be in the oven with just the pilot light left on, or on a very low setting with the door left slightly ajar. Alternatively you might try sitting the »

1.5 litres (52 fl oz/6 cups) full-cream (whole) milk

60 g (2½ oz/¼ cup) natural 'live' yoghurt (see note)

muslin (cheesecloth) (optional)

» jars in a small esky with warm water or place in a large saucepan with warm water, then cover with a lid and wrap the pan in blankets (or take it to bed with you …whatever works!) — you may need to be a little bit creative and try a few different options before you get it right. Place the jars in your 'incubator' and leave undisturbed for a minimum of 8 hours, after which time the yoghurt should be completely set. If it is still runny, return it to the incubator for a further 4 hours.

At this point the yoghurt is ready to eat but if you prefer it a bit thicker (Greek-style), transfer it into a colander or sieve lined with a few layers of muslin, place over a bowl and let it drain for 1 hour. (If you want to make labne you need to hang it for longer — see the variation at the end of this recipe.) Return to sterilised jars, seal and refrigerate for up to 10 days.

NOTE: *For your first batch, look for any yoghurt that has 'live cultures' on the label. Make sure to keep a few spoonfuls of your own yoghurt if it has turned out well, to use as your next starter culture. As long as you are making yoghurt every week, or more often, your culture will stay alive — this means that every subsequent batch becomes more of your own unique yoghurt.*

VARIATION: *To make labne, hang the yoghurt in the muslin-lined sieve set over a bowl for 24 hours, then drain the whey from the bowl and turn the yoghurt onto a fresh piece of muslin. Place back into the sieve over the bowl and drain for a further 24–48 hours, or until it weighs about 400 g (14 oz) — at this point it is still soft but rollable.*

YOGHURT

YOGHURT AND OLIVE OIL CAKE

Serves 8

Nick came by this recipe when he was studying in Adelaide and working in a Greek restuarant. The chef's mum used to bring it in, but it was impossible to get the recipe from her. This is a pretty good variation, without the ubiquitous snowfall of icing (confectioners') sugar. You can make it a bit more grown-up by splashing a few spoons of ouzo over it while it is cooling.

Preheat the oven to 180°C (350°F/Gas 4). Lightly grease and line the base and sides of a 20 x 10 x 6.5 cm (8 x 4 x 2½ inch) loaf (bar) tin with baking paper.

In a large bowl, sift together the flour, baking powder and salt.

In a separate bowl, rub together the sugar and lemon zest for a few minutes to coat the sugar in fragrant oil from the zest. Whisk in the yoghurt, eggs and vanilla. When the mixture is well blended, gently stir into the dry ingredients until smooth. Fold in the olive oil — the batter will be thick and shiny. Pour it into the tin and smooth the top.

Bake the cake for 50–55 minutes, or until it is golden — when a skewer inserted into the centre of the cake comes out clean it is ready. Allow to cool in the tin for 5 minutes, before turning out onto a wire rack to cool completely. Cut into slices and serve.

225 g (8 oz/1½ cups) plain (all-purpose) flour

2 teaspoons baking powder

a pinch of pure salt

220 g (7¾ oz/1 cup) caster (superfine) sugar

finely grated zest of 1 lemon

125 g (4½ oz/½ cup) natural 'live' yoghurt (pages 56–57)

3 free-range eggs, lightly beaten

¼ teaspoon natural vanilla extract

125 ml (4 fl oz/½ cup) extra virgin olive oil

SHANKLISH

Makes 2 balls

Shanklish is a traditional Levantine dish — it is a fresh cheese made from cow's, goat's or sheep's milk. Using labne to make this one is a bit of a cheat's way but you do get a great result. To make labne refer to the variation for the natural yoghurt on pages 56–57.

400 g (14 oz) labne (see variation for the natural 'live' yoghurt recipe on pages 56–57)

1 teaspoon ground cumin

a large pinch cayenne pepper

2 teaspoons pure sea salt flakes

1 bunch fresh mint, finely chopped

1 teaspoon dried chilli flakes, finely chopped

extra virgin olive oil

Remove the labne from the muslin and roll it into two balls. In a small bowl, combine the cumin, cayenne pepper, salt, mint and chilli flakes. Add the labne balls, one at a time, and roll to coat all over.

Arrange the balls on a serving plate, drizzle with a little olive oil and season with sea salt and freshly ground black pepper. Serve with bread and salad greens.

SAMOSAS

Makes 40 small samosas

Spiced potato and pea filling is fried in small pillowslips of yoghurt pastry to make these samosas. You could make a half batch if you're not feeding a mob, but for the work, a big batch makes more sense. In India they make half moons of pastry and fold into triangles, but we find a curry puff shape easier to prepare for less dexterous hands. They also make bigger samosas, which involves slightly thicker pastry.

FILLING

500 g (1 lb 2 oz) waxy potatoes

2 tablespoons ghee or vegetable oil

2 large onions, thinly sliced

a fat-thumb-sized piece of fresh ginger, grated

1 garlic clove, crushed

1 long green chilli, seeded if very hot and thinly sliced

1 tablespoon coriander seeds, toasted and crushed (see note)

2 teaspoons cumin seeds, toasted and crushed (see note)

1 teaspoon ground turmeric

1 teaspoon garam masala

200 g (7 oz) green peas (frozen is fine)

3 tablespoons chopped fresh coriander (cilantro) leaves

cayenne pepper (optional)

vegetable oil, for deep-frying

SAMOSA PASTRY

550 g (1 lb 4 oz/3⅔ cups) plain (all-purpose) flour

2 teaspoons pure sea salt

160 g (5½ oz) butter, melted to warm but not hot

160 g (5½ oz/⅔ cup) natural 'live' yoghurt (pages 56–57)

To make the pastry, mix together the flour and salt in a large bowl. Add the melted butter, yoghurt and just enough water to make a stiff dough, about 2 tablespoons (don't overdo the water — if you do, add more flour). Knead until smooth and stretchy. Set aside.

To make the filling, peel the potatoes, dice them into 5 mm (¼ inch) cubes and place them in a saucepan with enough water to cover. Bring to the boil and cook for 10 minutes, or until tender. Remove from the heat, drain and set aside.

Heat the ghee in a large heavy-based frying pan over medium heat. Add the onion and ginger and cook slowly until the onion starts to brown. Adding some salt at this early stage helps the onion brown more evenly and quickly. Toss in the garlic and chilli and continue frying for a further 1 minute. Make sure the heat is as low as it can go, then add the ground coriander and cumin seeds, the turmeric and garam masala and cook for 1 minute. Remove from the heat and stir in the potato, peas and fresh coriander. Mix all this up together and taste for salt and chilli, adding cayenne pepper or more chilli if you want more spice.

Roll out the dough to 3 mm (⅛ inch) thick and cut into 10 cm (4 inch) rounds using a cookie cutter or similar. Place a heaped tablespoon of the filling mixture on one half of each pastry round, moisten the edges with water, then fold the other side over and crimp to make a sealed parcel. This sealing is important for when you fry the samosas.

When ready to cook, pour enough vegetable oil into a saucepan or wok so it's about 3 cm (1¼ inches) deep. Heat the oil over high heat to about 180°C (350°F) — a cube of bread will sizzle immediately — and deep-fry the samosas, in batches, until brown, turning over when coloured on the underside. Remove with a slotted spoon and lay on kitchen paper to drain.

Dish them up while hot or warm and serve with fresh minted yoghurt, a green sauce made of mashed fresh coriander leaf and black salt, or some bought mango chutney.

NOTE: *To toast spices, dry-fry whole spices such as coriander, cumin and the like in a frying pan over low heat, tossing often until the spices change aroma. If you wait for them to darken in colour, they're probably burnt. It's best to toast each spice separately as their differing shapes and sizes mean they will toast at different speeds. Spices that are already ground are notoriously hard to roast as they scorch and go acrid very quickly.*

MEAT

MEAT

WHY, YOU MAY ASK IN A TIME OF UBIQUITOUS REFRIGERATION, BOTHER TO PRESERVE MEAT? OR MAKE YOUR OWN BANGERS WHEN EVERY BUTCHER WORTH THEIR FLOSSY SALT IS MAKING THEM?

Well, the reason is plain and simple: flavour. If you want something better than money can buy, something unique, tasting more of itself and unlike many commercial products that frequently take shortcuts, then doing it yourself fits the bill.

It's no wonder modern sausages have been termed 'surprise bags' for all the mystery meats that go into them. It's no wonder people are disappointed by bacon that leaches water and smells like fish when it is cooked. It's not surprising to realise that most people think that ham should taste like 'smoke flavour' instead of a smokehouse, when most of the stuff for sale has never actually been near real smoke or a flame.

Preserving your own meat is an inexact science, an endlessly rewarding project where the results are as individual as those who make them. Was it a wet winter? Then the prosciutto may be softer than last year. Is the pork for the bangers from a Wessex Saddleback rather than a Berkshire this time around? If so, the meat will be sweeter. Is the wood for smoking the bacon apple wood rather than eucalypt? The beef from a three-year-old rather than a 14-month-old steer? Everything changes, and with that change comes infinite possibility and variation. Get out the sausage cannon, fire up the smoker, ring up the butcher or kill the pig yourself and get prepared for the flavours of yesterday.

SMOKING

Curing is one way of preserving food, smoking it is another. However, without curing, smoking is relatively ineffectual and cured and smoked food lasts longer than either process alone. This is because the smoke acts in two ways: to dry the food and to sanitise (sterilise) the outside of it.

Smoking is both an art and a science, and good, consistent smoking can take years to perfect. The good news for the home smoker is that just about anything you smoke yourself will taste better than most of the stuff you buy. Partly it's because you know what goes into your food and can eat it shortly after smoking, and partly because so many 'smoked' products aren't actually smoked at all, just flavoured with a smoky-tasting chemical or residue.

The important things to think of when smoking are how you will cure the ingredient, whether you'll hot or cold smoke it, and what kind of smoke you'll create. Not only are various woods used, you can also use tea, sugar and anything natural that burns. But there are some limitations. For any kind of smoking you must not use resinous wood. This includes many soft woods, but in particular avoid using pine. Good hardwood isn't resinous, so the wood from most fruit trees is a good option as it produces a flavoursome smoke, each variety with its own unique properties. The wood for smoke is important, but you can control flavour just as much with the brine and cure. We use Tasmanian hardwood for much of our smoking because it's plentiful, cheap (free when we cut firewood) and works well with full-flavoured free-range old-breed pork.

Building your own smoker can be as rudimentary or as complicated as you want. An old biscuit tin can have holes punched through, be placed over a low flame and used to hot smoke small cuts or fish, such as trout or eel. A 44 gallon drum can be converted to a fire box by cutting holes near the base to let in air, then drilling smaller holes near the top to insert metal hanging rods. You can dodgy up a makeshift cold smoker using plywood to form a box, placing it on a raised platform, and having a separate fire pit with a metal flue to draw up the smoke into the box. Some people use old fridges as the smoker, or old cookers. All you need is a fairly enclosed space with some room for the smoke to draw out the top, and a place where you can have a small fire going that won't set the food (or the smoker!) alight. We've used little gas flames under metal tins, kettle-style barbecues for large cuts, and a loose structure of old bricks for smoking fish.

HOT SMOKING

The most difficult smoking to get right is actually hot smoking, because the heat of the fire can adversely affect the end result, so you're trying to balance the need for some heat, and some smoke, with the need to not create too much heat or smoke at any one time. The smoke comes straight from a fire and is captured under an enclosed lid and the food cooks as it smokes.

The down side of hot versus cold smoking is that the fat in hot smoked food can go rancid quicker than cold smoked meats. It also changes the texture of the meat, so it isn't always desirable for fish or other delicate textures. Despite its name, hot smoked food is ideally cooked at or around 100°C (200°F), so it's not particularly hot when compared to an oven. Hot smoked food should reach an internal temperature of at least 72°C (162°F) but work on 80°C (176°F) for safe home smoking.

In the old days people often smoked their bacon in the chimney above their fire. Hot smoking is perfect for ham, because it needs to be cooked at some point anyway. It also works really well for other ingredients that either benefit from their cooked texture, or aren't going to be cooked another time and need to be cooked before being eaten.

COLD SMOKING

Cold smoking, as the name suggests, means that smoke is cooled before it surrounds the food. This method doesn't cook the ingredient at all, and sometimes (as in bacon) the cooking will happen later. Some things, such as smoked fish, can be eaten raw. Cold smoking is more complicated to do at home because you need to have the food separated from the fire, either by distance or a pipe. Cold smoking is ideally done at temperatures around about 20°C (68°F), but can be done at higher temperatures if not done for too long at a time.

Cold-smoked products are generally subtler. Most salmon is cold smoked, hence the fine slivers and slippery texture. You can cold smoke food using less smoke for longer, which means you can control the smoke better. That said, to build a cold smoker takes more effort. A fire pit connected by a pipe to an old fridge or metal drum can work a treat. The idea is that the pipe is long enough to cool the smoke to a reasonably low level. Remember to leave some air holes at the top of your smoker to help draw the smoke up out of the fire, and often it's better to use subtler styles of wood.

HAM, PICKLED PORK AND PROSCIUTTO

You'd think, with every supermarket, every butcher, every corner store and every sandwich shop selling a version of ham, and often prosciutto as well, there's very little point in learning how to make it yourself. Until you've tasted properly cured and smoked pork leg, that is.

Ham, prosciutto and pickled pork all come from pigs' legs. You can, of course, make ham from a small cut from the shoulder (the scotch or neck), but generally, a cured part or whole leg is the aim. It's best to start with small cuts and build up from there. As always, choose meat from as good a pig as you can afford. We're lucky enough to have pigs from Matthew's and Ross's farms, both Wessex Saddleback and Berkshire breeds, that live happy, free-range lives. You may not have access to your own pasture-raised pork, but you'll be wasting your time trying to turn a poorly raised animal into something sublime. Curing and smoking can't restore what wasn't in the meat in the first place.

CLASSIC SMOKED ENGLISH-STYLE LEG HAM

Yields 5.5 kg (12 lb 6 oz)

Moist without being wet. Tender, smoky and rich from the flavour of the cure, sweet, good-quality pork can reach majestic status in the best ham. But the best ham is hardly available for sale these days. Big manufacturers often don't put the meat into a room with a fire under one end, but rather use a 'smoke flavour', which is reminiscent of liquid tar that can be ladled into the vat. They use 'binders' to hold water in the meat. They roll the legs in large machines not dissimilar to concrete mixers to massage the pork and make it absorb more moisture. They take a 7 kilogram (15 lb 12 oz) leg of fresh pork and inject it with soy bean proteins to sell you a 12 kilogram (27 lb) leg of ham, and all you get for the price is 5 kilograms (11 lb 4 oz) of salty water. Even small butchers can be found using binders and food colouring to make what really should be just a very simple piece of meat.

The way to make a smoked leg ham is best tried for the first time with a boned-out leg. That way, the cure can make it to all sides of the meat. A bone-in leg runs the risk that the cure may not reach the centre. Butchers use a long hollow needle to pump the cure into the centre but you don't necessarily need one if you have a very cold environment and can spend the time waiting for the meat to cure. The needle simply speeds up the process, though it can add water to the ham at the same time (a good thing for those selling ham, not for those buying it or eating it).

4.5–5 kg (10 lb 2 oz–11 lb 4 oz) boneless pork leg

butcher's twine

a way to smoke the ham (kettle-style barbecues work well, see pages 70–71)

CURING MIXTURE

500 g (1 lb 2 oz) pure sea salt

5 g (⅛ oz) sodium nitrate (see note, page 90)

3 g sodium erythorbate (see note, page 90)

To make the curing mixture, put 5 litres (175 fl oz) water in a large non-reactive tub or bucket (it has to be big enough to submerge the ham) with the salt, nitrate and erythorbate and mix until dissolved.

Stab the ham leg with a fine-bladed knife or wooden skewer in about 20 places, especially in the fattest part of the meat to help the cure penetrate. Place the pork leg in this brine and weigh it down to ensure it stays below the surface of the liquid. Cover, place in a cool, dark place (about 12°C/54°F) and leave for 1½ days per kilo of meat. (So 4.5 kg will take at least 6 days.)

Remove from the brine and tie firmly into a log using butcher's twine.

To smoke the ham, you can either hot smoke it, which is ideal if you can do it at a very low temperature, about 80–100°C (176–200°F) for 5 hours. Alternatively, you can cold smoke the ham (for the same amount of time) after it has first been poached in water until the internal temperature reaches 80°C (176°F) — whichever method you choose you need to cook the ham until the internal temperature reaches at least 75°C (167°F). You'll need to insert a meat thermometer into the fattest part of the cut, near the bone if you're doing a bone-in ham. Depending on how you are going with the smoking, if the meat is getting too smoky, or you're simply sick of managing the smoker after an hour or two, you could part smoke it and then speed it up by finishing the cooking in the oven.

Once the ham has smoked, allow it to sit for 1–3 days in the refrigerator before carving, to let the flavours settle a bit.

PICKLED PORK

Yields about 1.7 kg (3 lb 12 oz)

Pickled pork is, at its simplest, just a brined piece of raw pig flesh that you cook at home. Brine (salt and water) acts to preserve the meat and bring out more flavour through a complex chemical reaction that gets more flavoursome with time. Like most old ways of preserving, this one has survived to the modern day because it tastes terrific, too. You can pickle pork in a simple concoction, and add the flavourings later. It's possible to boil the pork with bay leaves, molasses, juniper berries or allspice. You can add mustard powder, thyme, garlic or beer, when it comes time to cook. We've given two ways to pickle pork — one for boiling, and the other for smoking a nitrate-free ham or baking the pork in a bed of hay.

Put 2 litres (70 fl oz/8 cups) water in a large non-reactive tub or bucket (it has to be big enough to submerge the pork) with the salt and mix well.

Place the pork in this brine and weigh it down to ensure it stays below the surface of the liquid. Cover, place in a cool, dark place (about 12°C/54°F) and leave for 4 days.

After this time, it's ready to simmer immediately. If you want to roast it, it needs soaking in cold water for a day first. Simmer for an hour in fresh water and you'll end up with a texture not dissimilar to ham, but without the smokiness. It's excellent served very simply, with boiled vegetables and Ross's wholegrain mustard (see page 248).

200 g (7 oz) pure sea salt

2 kg (4 lb 8 oz) piece of relatively lean pork, preferably from the neck (sometimes called pork 'scotch')

PICKLED PORK TO MAKE A NITRATE-FREE SMOKED HAM

Yields about 3 kg (6 lb 12 oz)

3 kg (6 lb 12 oz) boned-out
  pork leg

STOUT AND MOLASSES
  CURE
2 litres (70 fl oz/8 cups) stout
400 g (14 oz) molasses
400 g (14 oz) pure sea salt
12 bay leaves
20 whole cloves
2 cinnamon sticks
20 allspice seeds
butcher's twine

To make the stout and molasses cure, put 4 litres (70 fl oz/8 cups) water into a large non-reactive tub or bucket (it has to be large enough to submerge the pork) with the stout, molasses, salt and spices and stir until the salt has dissolved.

Place the pork in the brine mixture and weigh it down to ensure it stays below the surface of the liquid. Cover and leave to soak for 6 days in a cool, dark place (about 12°C/54°F).

Hang by tying with butcher's twine or a butcher's hook and suspending, preferably in a cool, dark but airy place for 1 day to dry (see page 91). You can then either use in dishes as is or continue to hang for a further month for the flavours to become more complex before cooking. You can also cold smoke for 6 hours as you would a classic smoked English-style leg ham (see pages 74–75).

PROSCIUTTO

Yields about 7 kg (15 lb 12 oz)

Air-dried ham has all sorts of names depending on where you first encountered it — prosciutto, jambon, jamón. There are many variations, some using smoke, some using red wine, but here is the simplest version where the leg is salt-cured (no nitrate) and hung to dry. In the right environment the leg could be matured for years, but plan on not touching it for six months and eating it at 12 months for most locations. It's important to use a big leg, preferably from a fat, female pig so it doesn't dry out and the meat is sweet at the start. It's far easier to find a place to hang a ham in temperate regions than it is in hotter climes, so adjust your curing, hanging and eating times accordingly.

Trim the pork leg well so it doesn't have any dags hanging off, or deep cuts. Cut it so it is rounded at the base. We like to give the meat a good beating at this stage, but a solid massage also works. To soften the meat, we give it a decent walloping with a wooden rolling pin for about 30–40 whacks, trying to give all the leg a bit of a seeing-to, avoiding any bony bits.

There is likely to be some blood in an artery that runs down the leg, and you can squeeze this out by pressing from the foot end up along the bone and towards the hip joint. Only a teaspoon or less will be there, and we mop it up using a bit of kitchen paper. Some people inject the artery with a brine solution from the foot end, to flush it out, but we find that hard to do and the pressing method is just as successful.

Take a large non-reactive tub, preferably one with a lid, and put some salt in the bottom. Place the leg in the tub and rub the salt liberally all over, particularly around the exposed »

10 kg (22 lb 8 oz) free-range pork leg, boned out to reveal ball joint

2–3 kg (4 lb 8 oz–6 lb 12 oz) medium-grain pure sea salt

lard, for smearing

coarsely ground black pepper

fly netting or fine cloth such as muslin (cheesecloth), to avoid insects

a swag of patience

» meat and ball joint area. Lay the leg, skin side down, in a bed of salt and cover the exposed meat with more salt. Place a weight on top of the leg (if you're curing two legs, let one weigh the other down, and swap them over each day) — about 5–8 kg (11 lb 4 oz–18 lb) of weight is good. You could use a flour bag or water containers, making sure you protect the leg from the weight using plastic wrap.

Keep the leg in this salt for about 15 days at 12°C (54°F) or below (allow 1½–2 days per kilo of meat), turning it and rubbing the slurry of salt over it as you go.

When the leg has cured, remove from the salt and wash it off. Many people use red wine vinegar to rub over the pork at this point to keep the surface sterile. Smear the open side of the meat well with enough lard to completely seal it.

Scatter coarsely ground black pepper on the lard and hang the leg in a cool place (12°C or below) — you want cool and humid rather than a coolroom, which is cool and dry (see page 91). In some areas you may need to cover the meat with fly netting, and always find a place that is away from rodents. Hang the meat for 6 months or even better 1 year. Ideally, it will get a bloom of white mould all over after a few weeks.

When ready to eat, scrub off the mould and the lard, perhaps trimming the outside of the meat. Carve off the skin and discard. Cut very fine slices of the ham and serve very simply, perhaps with fragrant melon, grissini or sweet summer figs.

MARMALADE AND MUSTARD BAKED HAM

Serves 16

Good ham, made the old-fashioned way, where it's hung for a bit after curing, and not pumped full of binding agents to absorb water, is best soaked overnight before baking. That way it doesn't become too dry (ham is already cooked before you buy it). If you buy a cheaper style ham with a binding agent, you probably want to cook the water out rather than soak it first.

6 kg (13 lb 8 oz) whole classic smoked English-style leg ham (pages 74–75), skin scored deeply into the fat in diamonds

2 x 750 ml (26 fl oz) bottles dry cider

6 pieces blade mace

100 g (3½ oz/½ cup) soft brown sugar

300 g (10½ oz) Seville orange marmalade

½ teaspoon mustard powder

Take the ham and soak it in a cider-flavoured stock overnight — use 1 bottle of the cider and enough water to cover (don't worry if the hock isn't completely under the water).

Remove the ham from the brine the next day and place in a deep roasting tin. Discard the soaking liquid (you could actually boil it down to add to the baste if you have the time and energy).

Preheat the oven to 150°C (300°F/Gas 2). Bring the remaining cider to the boil in a saucepan with the mace, sugar and marmalade. Simmer for 10 minutes, then add the mustard powder. Pour over the ham and cook in the oven for 2 hours, basting regularly with the juices from the tin. You may want to start the process with the ham covered to keep it moist, then remove the foil or lid for the last hour of cooking.

When the ham has warmed through (test the temperature next to the bone, it needs to be 70°C/158°F) and the marinade has started to thicken it is done — you can speed up the process by draining the juices from the tin and reducing them in a pan until thick and syrupy — if your roasting tin is the type that can stand some heat — do it in the tin on the stovetop.

Spoon the sauce over the hot ham. Serve with a bit of mustard, a warm potato salad (see page 253) and a glass of something good.

PICKLED PORK BAKED IN HAY

Serves 10–12

Baking in hay is an old method used to retain the moisture in meat. Cooked gently it will impart a beguiling herbaceous note. Good hay will smell sweet; don't use anything that smells mouldy or tired because this will flavour the pork. In the absence of a pickled pork leg, use a bought gammon leg or a leg of ham for a different but equally delicious result. Take care, however, not to let any of the hay poke out or it could catch fire and damage not only dinner, but your oven and the house.

If the pork or ham is salty, soak overnight in fresh water to draw out some of the cure. Remove from the water and wrap in the muslin — this will stop the hay sticking to the meat.

Preheat the oven to 150°C (300°F/Gas 2). Moisten the hay by splashing with water. Place a few handfuls of hay in the base of a roasting tin to line it well. Lay the pickled ham leg on top and cover with more hay — you want a 5 cm (2 inch) layer of loose hay on top and bottom at least. Seal the leg and hay into the tray using foil — you really want a good tight fit to keep the hay steaming in the foil and keep the meat moist.

Bake in the oven for about 3–4 hours, or until the meat is hot right through. Remove the foil, carefully scrape aside the hay and remove the meat from the muslin, being careful to unwrap it in a way that you won't get any hay or seeds on the meat.

Carve as you would a ham. You can serve the meat warm or cold, as the mood or occasion dictates, with mustard, relishes and pickles (see pages 219–228).

3 kg (6 lb 12 oz) pork leg, brined using the stout and molasses cure on page 77

muslin (cheesecloth), for wrapping

several good handfuls clean hay, preferably including some lucerne

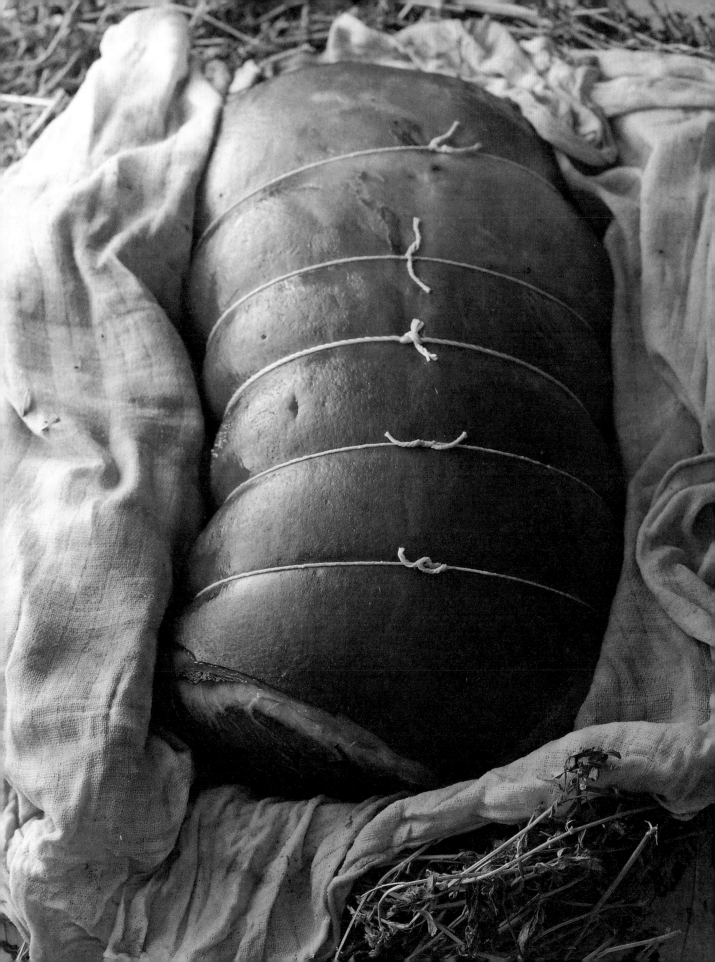

PROSCIUTTO AND ROCKET PIZZA

Makes 2 thin pizzas

Homemade prosciutto is almost too good to cook with, but thrown on top of a pizza hot from the oven you get the best of the flavour. Ideally, you can use the hotplate of a covered barbecue to cook the pizza — it's hotter than an oven and can darken the base nicely, though the tops stay pale. If you make the dough a day or two ahead you don't have to knead it. If you're in a hurry, use warm water (not so hot you can't put your hand in it), and knead it more, don't put it in the fridge then use when it's doubled in size.

250 ml (9 fl oz/1 cup) tomato passata (puréed tomatoes)

2 purple garlic cloves, crushed

3–4 fresh basil leaves

2½ tablespoons extra virgin olive oil, plus extra for brushing

16 young tender rocket leaves, washed, dried and torn

10 thin slices prosciutto (pages 78–79) or pancetta (page 97)

PIZZA DOUGH

300 g (10½ oz/2 cups) plain (all-purpose) flour

2 teaspoons (7 g sachet) dried yeast

1 teaspoon salt

1 teaspoon sugar

olive oil, for drizzling

To make the dough, mix together the flour, yeast, salt and sugar in a bowl. Make a well in the centre, pour in 200 ml (7 fl oz) water and mix with a spoon until it's too hard to stir, then finish mixing with your hand to make a smooth dough. Sprinkle in a little more flour if needed. Knead for 5 minutes. Form into a ball, rub all over with olive oil, place into a large bowl, cover with plastic wrap and refrigerate for a couple of hours.

Meanwhile, put the passata, garlic, basil and olive oil in a saucepan, season with salt and pepper and simmer for 10 minutes. If it gets too thick, add a splash of water. Set aside to cool.

Preheat the oven to 230°C (450°F/Gas 8) or as hot as it can get. If you have a pizza stone use that (following the manufacturer's instructions). Divide the pizza dough into two even portions and roll out each portion on a sheet of baking paper to make thin rounds. Brush with a little olive oil and smear the tomato sauce over the top.

Transfer the pizza rounds onto flat trays lined with baking paper (or the pizza stone) and bake towards the top of the oven for about 5–10 minutes. Just try to get them to darken slightly on the bases. Top with the rocket leaves and lay over the thinly sliced prosciutto. Cut into quarters and serve immediately.

BACON

Bacon, in the pure sense, can mean simply the raw middle of a pig, boned out, though these days it's more likely to mean a cured, smoked middle, which is then sliced and fried to have with eggs. There are as many types of bacon as there are methods of curing and flavouring — honey or brown sugar cured, apple wood or hickory smoked. The big differences come in either dry curing (or nitrate-free curing) or brining and in hot or cold smoking. Like anything that's been smoked, the hot-smoked version will go rancid more rapidly because the fat has been heated once already.

CURING

When you cure meat, you're simply preserving it, using salt and sometimes a few trace chemicals to help prevent the growth of dangerous bacteria (such as botulism) and to introduce other subtle flavours. In the old days they used saltpetre, a salt of potassium nitrate (curiously enough, famed as an oxidiser in gunpowder) because it helped cure food far more efficiently than salt alone. Nowadays, we know that saltpetre is less consistent than some other food additives, so modern foods often use things like sodium nitrite or sodium nitrate in a strictly controlled fashion (they've also been shown to be more effective in controlling bacterial growth). Saltpetre is still an approved food additive in much of the world, and some swear it gives a better end result in terrines and salami.

One of the other effects of all three additives is that they cause the meat to stay pink, even when cooked, hence the colour of bacon compared to a piece of cooked pork. We've heard of an organic butcher doing nitrate-free ham and having his customers reject it simply because of its grey colour.

There is another effect of the curing agents on the body. The nitrate is converted to nitrite in the process, and both nitrite and nitrate become nitrosamines when digested, and nitrosamines are a suspected carcinogen. Used in minute quantities, and eaten in moderation, there's little risk to most people, but an increasing number of people like to avoid the additives for health reasons. There are some associations between nitrosamines produced in the body when they're eaten and diabetes, Alzheimer's and Parkinson's disease, too. Eating foods cured without nitrate or nitrite doesn't mean you'll avoid this, however. Some 'natural' food additives such as celery powder have the same effect on meat, and on the body, and even salt-cured food can have some quantity of nitrate/nitrite in it. We like to do some nitrate-free curing because it means a slower cure, a truer meat flavour, and we think limiting added nitrates to your diet probably isn't a bad thing. You can buy sodium nitrate and sodium erythorbate from some butchers or butchers' supply shops, though for home use a friendly butcher will probably supply a smaller amount than the 1 kg (2 lb 4 oz) tubs often bought by the professionals.

Nitrate-free curing is simpler for the home curer and for that we recommend a simple sea salt, with no anti-caking agent. Most salt sold for the house has a chemical added that stops it clumping, and while it's debatable whether it has much effect on curing, purists prefer a pure sea salt. For most uses a coarse salt is fine, though a fine table salt cures more quickly. Butchers use a coarse salt, sometimes called 'flossy salt' because of its fine threadlike texture.

HANGING YOUR PRODUCTS

They say that if you want to be happy for a week, get married. If you want to be happy for a month, kill a pig, and if you want to be happy for a lifetime, plant a garden. While there's a lot of truth in that, killing a pig means meat for more than just one month if you cure it. Because this book is all about the preservation of food, you'll be well advised to have a place in mind to hang things, as meat — even a simple bacon and ham — usually improve with hanging after curing.

The best place to hang food is in a cellar or the equivalent — somewhere about 12°C (54°F), that has some humidity, is airy but isn't subject to a breeze. In temperate climes, such as Tasmania where we live, we can get away with hanging our meats in a barn or shed in the cooler months. All we need to do is to rodent-proof the top, to protect the meat from wasps and flies — muslin (cheesecloth), shade cloth or even some soft fly mesh work well — and hang things in the cooler, wetter months from May to October.

Hanging outside of these months, particularly when a product is fresh (such as prosciutto) is more difficult and requires a bit more thought. You can humidify a space by hanging wet towels in it. This also helps to cool the room. But if you live in a warm climate with no access to a cellar, you're better to mature things in a fridge or coolroom, taking care to keep the humidity up. By nature, fridges and coolrooms dry the air, making for dry-cured meats. Because we don't live in a warmer climate, we haven't had to come up with novel ways to cure meats, but underneath the house, out of the breeze, in the coolest, moistest spot is going to work best in most places. Use nature to your advantage, and only try to hang products when the weather is going to be on your side.

Once you've found a place to hang your salami or speck, the trick is to get a hole through part of the meat and insert a hanging hook. We've found the best place to hang things is from a hook that is screwed into the ceiling to avoid rats and mice.

AMERICAN BACON

Yields about 4 kg (9 lb)

American bacon is made from the streaky end of the pork middle. This is the belly bit, but doesn't include the loin, and is intended to be cooked until crisp. In much of the United States bacon is cured with a sweetener, perhaps with sugar or maple syrup or similar. If you want to make less, adapt the quantities of curing liquid to the amount of bacon you want to make.

Put 5 litres (175 fl oz) water in a large non-reactive tub (it has to be big enough to submerge the pork) with the salt, sugar, sodium nitrate and sodium erythorbate and mix until it has dissolved. Add the pork belly, and leave in a cold place for 3 days, ideally in the refrigerator.

When cured, remove the meat and hang to dry overnight (see page 91). Cold smoke the bacon for about 3 hours and it should be ready to use immediately, though it's better after a couple of days.

500 g (1 lb 2 oz) pure sea salt

300 g (10½ oz) sugar, honey or maple syrup, or use a combination

5 g (⅛ oz) sodium nitrate (see note, page 90)

5 g (⅛ oz) sodium erythorbate (see note, page 90)

4 kg (9 lb) piece of pork belly

GREEN BACON

Yields about 4 kg (9 lb)

Green bacon is simply unsmoked, cured pork middle. For the start of its life, it is cured in the same way a ham or bacon is, but it's not cooked or smoked and finished in the same way. In reality you can use the same cure for gammon, ham, green bacon and smoked bacon — throw all the cuts into the same brine tub and just remove them when they're done. You then alter the flavour by how you cook/smoke/bake the finished result.

4 kg (9 lb) boned-out pork middle, including loin

1 portion curing mixture from classic smoked English-style leg ham (pages 74–75)

Simply cure the meat in the curing bath as you would the ham, allowing 2 days per kilogram. When done, hang the meat to dry for 1 week in a cool, airy place below 12°C/54°F (see page 91). For variation, you can try substituting cider for some of the water in the cure.

CLASSIC COLD-SMOKED BACON

Yields about 4 kg (9 lb)

A good cold smoked bacon is simply a green bacon that is smoked and, ideally, left to hang for a week before being sliced ready to fry.

1 side green bacon, straight from the cure (see above)

Cold smoke the bacon for about 4 hours, or until done to your liking (pages 70–71). Hang it for 1 week once smoked to dry the flesh and let the flavours settle (see page 91). Slice thick or thin and be sure to crisp the rind for eating, too.

DRY-CURED, NITRATE-FREE BACON

Yields about 3 kg (6 lb 12 oz)

At their Rare Food market stall in Hobart, Matthew and Ross occasionally sell a dry-cured nitrate-free bacon. It's done with a salt and sugar cure and avoids the nasties that so many find affect their health — added sodium nitrate and sodium nitrite. At its best, this bacon is sweet, rich, smoky and glorious. At its worst it is very hard to cut, extremely salty and best used in small amounts in soups, pasta sauces or casseroles.

In a large bowl, combine the salt and sugar. Sprinkle liberally in the base of a large non-reactive tub that is big enough to fit the pork middle, cutting the pork if that makes more sense to cover the base.

Rub some more of the salt mixture over the pork and rub in well on all sides and edges. Lay the pork, skin side down, in the tub. Use the rest of the salt mixture to spread over the meat, then cover it well to keep out insects. Allow this meat to cure for 3–4 days in a cool place, ideally the refrigerator, making sure to rub the salt and sugar 'slurry' over the meat and turn over each day.

After the meat has cured, rinse off the sugar and hot or cold smoke (see pages 70–71).

600 g (1 lb 5 oz) pure coarse sea salt

400 g (14 oz) soft brown sugar

4 kg (9 lb) piece of boned-out pork middle, including loin

WET-CURED, NITRATE-FREE BACON

Yields about 4 kg (9 lb)

You can make a nitrate-free, brine-cured bacon, too, which doesn't run the risk of being as salty as the dry-cured one.

200 g (7 oz) pure coarse sea salt

4 kg (9 lb) piece of boned-out pork middle, including loin

Put 2 litres (70 fl oz/8 cups) water into a large non-reactive tub that is big enough to fit the pork, and add the salt, stirring to dissolve. Place the pork in this brine and weigh it down to ensure it stays below the surface of the liquid. Cover, place in a cool, dark place (about 12°C/54°F) and leave the pork in this brine — allowing 1 day per kilogram of meat, more if it's very fatty pork. Smoke as per other bacons, either hot or cold (see pages 70–71).

SPECK

Yields about 2 kg (4 lb 8 oz)

Speck is a cured piece of boned-out rump (or sometimes belly) not dissimilar to bacon really, but one that is matured over a long time rather than quickly cured, after being heavily and repeatedly smoked. Often it is hung for a month or two to ripen naturally after being salt cured (no nitrates), then cold smoked. Traditionally it has quite a high juniper content compared to other cured and smoked pork meat.

Mix together the salt, sugar, juniper berries, bay leaves and thyme in a large bowl. Sprinkle liberally in the base of a large non-reactive tub that is big enough to fit the pork rump, cutting the pork if that makes more sense to cover the base. Rub some more of the salt mixture over the pork and rub in well on all sides and edges. Lay the pork, skin side down, in the tub. Spread the rest of the salt mixture over the meat and cover well to keep out insects. Allow this meat to cure for 4 days in a cool place, ideally the refrigerator, making sure to rub the salt and sugar 'slurry' over the meat each day.

After the meat has cured, rinse off the salt mixture and cold smoke for about 2 hours every day for 5 days (see pages 70–71), hanging in an airy, cool, dark, insect-free room between smokings (see page 91). Hang the finished speck for about 1 month before using in soups, sauces, or thinly sliced on pizza or over chicken prior to roasting.

600 g (1 lb 5 oz) pure coarse sea salt

400 g (14 oz) soft brown sugar

80 g (2¾ oz) juniper berries, crushed roughly using a mortar and pestle

8 fresh bay leaves

2 fresh thyme sprigs

3 kg (6 lb 12 oz) piece of boned-out pork rump

PANCETTA

Yields about 1.5 kg (3 lb 5 oz)

Pancetta is a very simple cured piece of pork belly that can be made using salt and simple spices and herbs you'd find in supermarkets. Most regions of Italy do a version and the spicing varies with the location. It's used mostly in pasta sauces — carbonara and amatriciana are the most famed if you don't have guanciale (cured pig cheek) and the like — though you might find pancetta on a pizza or draped over quail or chicken in place of bacon. It gets better by being hung for six weeks, but we've found you can start carving off chunks around the two-week mark if you're impatient. The problem with that is you reduce the amount of really good stuff you'll eat later.

---

20 fresh sage leaves

2 small fresh rosemary sprigs

20 whole black peppercorns

2 whole nutmeg

200 g (7 oz) medium-grain pure sea salt

2 kg (4 lb 8 oz) piece of pork belly

Place half of the sage, rosemary and peppercorns in a mortar. Finely grate 1 nutmeg on top and use a pestle to pound until a coarse paste is formed. Add ½ teaspoon of the salt if needed to get it to grind up well. Stir this herb mixture into the remaining salt to combine.

Put the pork belly in a large non-reactive tub and rub over the salt mixture. Leave to cure for 3 days in the refrigerator. (You will also need to refrigerate the remaining herbs separately).

When the pork has cured, rinse off the salt, then place the remaining sage, rosemary and peppercorns in a mortar. Finely grate over the remaining nutmeg and use a pestle to pound to a coarse paste. You may need to add another ½ teaspoon salt to get it to grind up really well.

Massage the herb mixture into the meat so it goes into the whole open side (you won't be able to get it to stick to the skin, so don't bother). Leave to hang in a cool, airy but not breezy place for about 4 weeks, although 6 weeks is preferable (see page 91).

CURLY ENDIVE SALAD WITH LARDONS AND PICKLED EGG

Serves 4

This rich salad is a meal in itself. In the absence of pickled eggs, you could use hard-boiled or poached eggs instead. You could use the bacon fat to make the croutons. We would.

100 g (3½ oz) dry-cured nitrate-free bacon (page 94) or pancetta (page 97), cut into batons (lardons)

2 handfuls curly endive (frisée), washed and torn into moderate-sized pieces

100 g (3½ oz) croutons (see note)

Matthew's vinaigrette dressing (page 257)

2 beetroot (beets), simmered until tender, peeled, then cut into eighths and kept warm

4 pickled pub eggs (page 243), quartered

Heat the bacon in a large frying pan over medium heat and fry gently until it starts to surrender its fat. While it cooks, assemble the rest of the salad.

Toss the frisée with the croutons and enough vinaigrette to lightly coat the leaves. Taste for salt and pepper, though remember the bacon will be salty. Divide between four large flat bowls and dot the beetroot and eggs evenly around each one. Just before you eat, spoon the bacon over the salad, including some of the fat, and eat while warm.

NOTE: *To make the croutons, dice some white bread, toss it in olive oil to coat and cook in a 180°C (350°F/Gas 4) oven for about 10–15 minutes, tossing and turning often, or until crisp.*

BRAISED CHICKEN WITH BACON, PEAS AND TARRAGON

Serves 5–6

A good use for a salty dry-cured bacon or even speck, this dish speaks of quality ingredients. You could use pretty much any of your cured pork in this and it would taste fantastic.

Heat the butter in a large, preferably cast-iron, saucepan over low heat and fry the bacon until it surrenders its fat. Add the chicken and gently brown on all sides. Remove the chicken pieces and bacon using a slotted spoon and set aside.

In the same pan, cook the onion until soft, but try not to brown it. Return the chicken and bacon to the pan, pour in the wine and sprinkle in half of the tarragon. Increase the heat and boil vigorously for 5 minutes, or until the wine has lost its strong alcohol smell, then add 250 ml (9 fl oz/1 cup) water and bring to the boil again. Reduce the heat to low, cover, and simmer for about 45 minutes (or you can do this in an oven at 180°C/350°F/Gas 4). At this point, season with salt and pepper.

Tip in the peas (they can be straight from the freezer) and add the risoni. The only thing to watch is that there's enough liquid — the risoni will double in size, absorbing its own weight in water. If there's not enough liquid, add another 125 ml (4 fl oz/½ cup) or so of water. Stir as the mixture comes back to the boil to stop the risoni from sticking to each other or the base of the pan. Continue to cook until the risoni is tender and the chicken is cooked. Just before serving, add the remaining tarragon, check for salt and pepper, then serve with bread.

50 g (1¾ oz) butter

100 g (3½ oz) bacon (pages 92–95), cut into batons

1 large (about no. 20) free-range chicken, jointed (or equivalent bits)

1 large red onion, diced

500 ml (17 fl oz/2 cups) dry white wine

2–3 tablespoons fresh tarragon leaves

300 g (10½ oz/2 cups) peas (frozen is fine)

100 g (3½ oz) risoni (rice-shaped pasta)

PASTRAMI AND BRESAOLA

While it's pork that generally gets preserved, it's not the only meat that is cured and hung. In western China they have beef 'hams', giant cured chunks of cow leg that meet the religious needs of the mostly Muslim indigenous communities. In Italy you'll find cured goats' legs. We've seen duck 'prosciutto' and the like, too.

The two most commonly found cured cuts of beef in Australia (after corned beef) are pastrami and bresaola. From northern Italy, bresaola is a wine-cured chunk of beef that is then air-dried. Some expat Italians prefer it to prosciutto not only for its different flavour, but because you can cure it in a month not a year. Pastrami is spiced and smoked, and tastes its best as it comes from the smoker. Both can be sliced very thinly, and like all good cured meat, a little goes a long way. Use them a bit as you would prosciutto, adding to a braised leek dish as it comes from the stove, laid over a pizza in place of the prosciutto (see page 87), in a warm cheddar toastie with mustard and some pickled onions. Just use them and you'll be curing a second batch much sooner than you think.

BRESAOLA

Makes 2 x 325 g (11½ oz) pieces

This bresaola recipe is Ross's favourite. It is not clear if it is a traditional recipe or not because every time he asks an Italian they always give a different answer or no answer at all, leading him to believe that he's on the right track. You'll need a bucket and 3 metres of muslin (cheesecloth) for this one.

With the back of a large cooking knife give the juniper berries, garlic, thyme and rosemary a bit of a whack so they can release the flavours in the marinade. Transfer to a non-reactive bowl with the bay leaves and olive oil and stir to combine. Add the beef and rub the mixture all over. Place the beef and marinade in a small non-reactive tub or bucket. Add the red wine, place a plate over the top to submerge the beef completely — the oil will float to the top and act as a seal. Cover and refrigerate for 2 weeks.

Take the beef out and rub the sea salt all over, then wrap in muslin and tie with butcher's twine. Hang the beef in a cool, well-ventilated area for about 3 weeks at 14°C (57°F). If you live in a hotter climate, refrigerate the beef and allow a little longer for the curing process — up to 3 weeks.

7 juniper berries

3 purple garlic cloves

3 fresh thyme sprigs

2 fresh rosemary sprigs

2 bay leaves

2 tablespoons olive oil

1 kg (2 lb 4 oz) piece topside beef, excess fat trimmed and cut into two rectangular pieces

3 litres (105 fl oz) full-bodied red wine

4 tablespoons pure sea salt flakes

muslin (cheesecloth), for wrapping

butcher's twine

PASTRAMI

Makes 1.5 kg (3 lb 5 oz)

Pastrami is an extension of corned beef. After the brining process corned beef is boiled and served, while pastrami is made by then covering the meat with spices and hot smoking it. We have found that other meats, such as venison and wallaby also work well, and we tend to lean towards cooking them as they are low in fat and have a depth of flavour that you don't find in beef. Traditionally, any cut of beef was used to make pastrami, but these days brisket is most often used as it retains more moisture.

---

2 kg (4 lb 8 oz) piece of beef, venison or wallaby topside

3 tablespoons whole black peppercorns

3 tablespoons coriander seeds

BRINE

400 g (14 oz) pure sea salt

250 g (9 oz) sugar

80 g (2¾ oz) leatherwood honey

5 purple garlic cloves

2 tablespoons freshly ground black pepper

2 tablespoons ground black mustard seeds

2 tablespoons ground allspice

2 tablespoons ground mace

1 tablespoon dried chilli flakes (optional)

Combine all of the brine ingredients and 4 litres (140 fl oz) water in a stockpot or large saucepan and bring to the boil. Once the salt and sugar have dissolved, remove from the heat and allow to cool.

Place the meat in a large non-reactive tub or bucket. Pour the cold brine over the meat and then place a plate and a weight over the meat to keep it fully submerged. Refrigerate for 3 days.

Remove the meat from the brine, discarding the brine, and pat dry with kitchen paper. Set aside.

Put the peppercorns and coriander seeds in a dry frying pan over low heat and cook for 2–3 minutes, or until toasted. Remove from the heat and grind them in a spice grinder (they do not have to be too fine, a little chunky is good). Alternatively, you can grind them using a mortar and pestle.

Roll the meat in the pepper mixture and then place in your smoker. Hot smoke on 120°C (250°F) for 1–2 hours — you want the meat to reach an internal temperature of 72°C (162°F) to render it safe to eat. Once cooked you can eat the pastrami hot or cool it down to use as cold cuts.

REUBEN SANDWICH

Serves 4

This is one of the best uses for your homemade pastrami. It's a great sandwich for late poker nights, easy to make and eat and also great with beer.

40 g (1½ oz) butter

8 slices rye bread

8 slices gruyère cheese

350 g (12 oz) thinly sliced pastrami (page 107)

250 g (9 oz) sauerkraut (page 227)

½ cup Russian dressing (below)

RUSSIAN DRESSING

85 g (3 oz/⅓ cup) mayonnaise

1½ tablespoons Grandpa Steve's tomato sauce (ketchup) (page 242)

1½ teaspoons grated fresh horseradish (or horseradish in a jar but not horseradish cream)

½ teaspoon worcestershire sauce

To make the Russian dressing, combine all of the ingredients in a bowl then season with sea salt and freshly ground black pepper. Set aside.

This sandwich is assembled before you cook it. Butter one side of four slices of the bread, and place the slices, butter side down. Top each with a slice of gruyère cheese and then divide half of the pastrami among them. Squeeze out any excess moisture from the sauerkraut using kitchen paper. Divide the sauerkraut among the sandwiches, and top each one with a tablespoon of the Russian dressing. Add another layer of pastrami and a second slice of gruyère. Butter the remaining bread and place on top, butter side up.

Warm up a frying pan or barbecue hotplate and start to cook the sandwiches until they are golden brown, flipping them with a spatula to cook both sides. Cut each sandwich in half and serve hot.

CONFIT, RILLETTES, PÂTÉ AND TERRINE

Ooh là là — this is our French side coming out. The salt-cured meats of France have long inspired us on our respective travels, and nothing compares to the sublime flavour of a good confit or terrine.

At home we often confit things, salt curing them and braising them in their own fat, or pork fat, as is our wont. We do rabbit more often than the common duck confit, in the absence of legally killed and commercially available Tasmanian ducks. The process for all confit is the same, an overnight cure with salt, then a slow cook the next day. You can confit pork belly, goose, even lamb shoulder if you like. Remember, all these dishes are rich, so you'll only need a relatively small amount of them per serve.

113

RABBIT CONFIT

Serves 4

Confit is one of the age-old techniques of curing and storing meat for long periods of time. It is first salted then cooked in fat and stored in the fat until it is used. The main meats that are used are duck, goose and pork, although rabbit is also becoming popular. This procedure does take a couple of days so make sure you have the time set aside. If you decide to use farmed rabbit over wild then it will cook in half the time.

2 wild rabbits (about 800 g/
1 lb 12 oz each) or 1 farmed
rabbit (about 1–1.4 kg/
2 lb 4 oz–3 lb 2 oz)

200 g (7 oz) pure sea salt

2 bay leaves

½ bunch fresh thyme

1 tablespoon freshly ground
black pepper

4 French shallots, peeled and
sliced

5 purple garlic cloves

3 large waxy potatoes, such as
pink-eye, cut into 5 mm
(¼ inch) slices

500 g (1 lb 2 oz) rendered pork
fat or use 1 kg (2 lb 4 oz) duck
or goose fat

Find a large stockpot or saucepan that will hold the rabbit and have enough depth to cover with fat, which can also go in the oven — cast-iron is best. If you have to cut the rabbit into bits so be it, you will be taking the meat off the bone once it is cooked anyway. Place the rabbit into a non-reactive bowl and cover with the salt, turning to coat evenly. Cover and refrigerate for 12 hours.

Preheat the oven to 135°C (250°F/ Gas 1). Remove the rabbit from the refrigerator and rinse it under cold water. Pat dry with kitchen paper and place in the pot with all of the remaining ingredients, except the fat.

In a separate saucepan, melt the fat until it is pouring consistency, then pour it over the rabbit in the pot.

Put the rabbit over low heat and bring almost to the boil — try not to boil it as it will be tough if it cooks too quickly. Transfer the pot to the oven and cook it for 5 hours, checking it each hour after the first 3 hours have passed — when cooked the meat should fall easily from the bone. (If you are using farmed rabbit you will only need to cook it for 2–3 hours.) Once the rabbit is cooked then remove from the oven and set aside to cool.

Take the rabbit and strip the meat from the bones, discarding the bones and placing the flesh into a non-reactive bowl. Strain the fat and vegetables, and remove and discard the bay leaves. You can keep the fat for future confit and also for roasting meat and vegetables. (If you are making the confit rabbit and potato pie on page 123 you will need to add the vegetables back to the rabbit meat and stir to combine before filling the pie.)

To serve, heat the confit rabbit and potatoes in a hot oven until warm and crisp, then shred the meat through a salad or serve simply with vegetables.

NOTE: *If making a duck confit, follow the recipe above but omit the potato and French shallots if you are not making the pies.*

RILLETTES

Makes 10 x 110 g (3¾ oz) jars

Rillettes have become a major part of our life. For the past four years Ross has been making rillettes week in and week out for the Rare Food market stall. Like confit, it is a way of salt preserving meat but is more of a meat-style pâté. It is cooked for a long time in fat and a little stock until it is so tender that you can shred it to form a paste. Like confit, it can be made using duck, goose, pork, rabbit and varieties of fish. In France it is kept in tins for two or more years and most people would have at least one or more types in their cupboard. Unfortunately, in Australia it is not easy to set up a small cannery, the type that are so common in France. Our way of keeping it is to seal it in sterilised glass jars, which keeps them safe in the refrigerator for a couple of months. Rillettes are best eaten at room temperature on toast with cornichons or other pickles. Belly pork is commonly used for rillettes, but we use shoulder as it has a better texture and flavour. You have to leave the meat to sit overnight with the salt, so plan this one ahead.

1 kg (2 lb 4 oz) free-range
   pork shoulder, skin on

200 g (7 oz) pure sea salt

500 g (1 lb 2 oz) rendered duck
   or goose fat

STOCK

2 kg (4 lb 8 oz) pork bones

1 purple garlic bulb, halved

10 whole black peppercorns

5 juniper berries

2 bay leaves

1 bunch fresh thyme

Cut the pork shoulder into fist-sized pieces and place them in a plastic container. Rub the salt generously over the pieces of pork, cover and refrigerate for 12 hours.

Preheat the oven to 220°C (425°F/ Gas 7). To make the stock, place the pork bones in a roasting tin and cook them in the oven for 45 minutes, or until they are golden brown. Remove from the oven then transfer the bones to a stockpot or large saucepan and pour in enough water to cover the bones. Add all of the remaining stock ingredients and bring to the boil. Skim off any impurities, then reduce the heat to low and cook for 3–4 hours. Remove from the heat, strain the stock, discarding the bones and flavourings, and set aside.

Remove the pork from the refrigerator and rinse off the salt then pat dry with kitchen paper. Place the pork in a stockpot or large saucepan with the duck fat. Add enough of the stock to cover the meat — any leftover stock can be frozen for later use. Bring to the boil, then reduce the heat to low and simmer for about 4–6 hours, or until the meat breaks up easily — check by grabbing it with cooking tongs and pinching them together, if the meat breaks up easily then it is cooked.

Pull the meat out of the pot using a slotted spoon and place in a non-reactive bowl. Strain the liquid and set aside separately to cool down. Once the pork has cooled, remove and discard the skin, keep the fat from next to the skin and shred the meat and fat using two forks (or you can use clean hands) until it has a paste-like texture. Divide between 10 sterilised glass jars (see page 4) so that each is filled to about 7 mm (³⁄₈ inch) from the top of the jar. Take the reserved cooking liquid — use a ladle and make sure you get a mixture of stock and fat to top up the jars and fill all the air pockets. Seal with tight-fitting lids. You can reserve and refrigerate any extra liquor and use again — essentially creating a rillettes masterstock.

Lay a tea towel (dish towel) in the base of a very large stockpot or saucepan — this will stop the jars from rattling in the pan. Place the jars in a single layer on the tea towel, then fill the pot with enough fresh water so the jars are at least 2 cm (³⁄₄ inch) below the surface. Bring to the boil, then reduce the heat and simmer steadily for 2 hours. Remove from the heat, and when the jars are cool enough to handle, remove them from the pot and set aside to cool.

Store the rillettes in the refrigerator for up to 1 month or 1 week after opening. Serve at room temperature (stir to combine the fat, stock and the meat) with pickled onions, dill pickles and some crusty bread.

LIVER PÂTÉ

Serves 12

Pâté is one of those dishes that everyone would remember their mum bringing out at dinner parties. Then for a few days afterwards all of the kids got to fight over it for breakfast on toast. Recently, Ross had access to extra rabbit livers and made a parfait (a fancier version) but it wasn't cutting it, so he went back to this old faithful pâté recipe and then could not make enough of it to keep up with sales. We usually use rabbit livers to make this pâté, but if you can get chicken or duck a lot easier then go for it and see for yourself which one you like best.

Heat half of the butter in a large frying pan over low heat. Add the onion, garlic, thyme and rosemary and cook for 5 minutes, or until the onion softens without colouring. Add the livers and cook for a further 5 minutes, then add the port, sherry, Marsala and most of the remaining butter, reserving a tiny bit for the top. Stir until the butter melts, then transfer to a food processor and process to a smooth paste.

Pour the mixture into a serving mould (if entertaining a nice old mousse mould would be good or just use individual moulds or ramekins even). Melt the remaining butter and allow to cool, then pour over the pâté to seal the top. Refrigerate for at least 3 hours before serving with a side salad and toast or crackers.

375 g (13 oz) butter

2 brown onions, chopped

2 purple garlic cloves, crushed

3 fresh thyme sprigs

1 fresh rosemary sprig

500 g (1 lb 2 oz) rabbit, chicken or duck livers, trimmed

2 tablespoons port

2 tablespoons dry sherry

2 tablespoons Marsala

TERRINE

Makes 1.2 kg (2 lb 10 oz)

For the average person, terrine is the fanciest meatloaf that you have ever had. The list is endless with what you can use in a terrine, but this recipe relies on one thing: the best free-range pork you can buy, and if you can get old-breed pork all the better. If you are using this recipe to make pâté en croûte — see pages 124–125 — you will need collapsible pâté en croûte moulds or if you can't find any a loaf (bar) tin will do. You can use a terrine tin for this but you have to be very careful taking the terrine out — if you rip it then your jelly will run out and it just won't be the same.

1.5 kg (3 lb 5 oz) free-range pork shoulder, skin removed

5 French shallots, peeled

3 purple garlic cloves

1 handful fresh flat-leaf (Italian) parsley leaves

2 fresh thyme sprigs

2 fresh rosemary sprigs

15 g (½ oz) pure sea salt

10 g (¼ oz) freshly ground black pepper

Cut the pork into strips to make them easier to mince and place with all the other ingredients in a stainless steel bowl. Remove the sanitised mincer from the freezer (see page 134) and assemble it as per the manufacturer's instructions. Using a medium-sized disc, grind the mixture into a stainless steel bowl that has been sanitised and kept in the freezer. We like our terrine a little bit coarse but if you want it finer just put it through a second time.

Preheat the oven to 150°C (300°F/Gas 2). Line a 28 x 11 x 7.5 cm (11¼ x 4¼ x 3 inch) terrine mould with plastic wrap, making sure there is enough overhang to cover the top once filled. Press the mixture into the mould with some pressure so there are no air bubbles. Cover with the excess plastic wrap and then a layer of foil.

Place the mould into a deep baking tray with enough water to come halfway up the sides. Cook the terrine in the oven for 75 minutes. Remove the terrine and set aside to cool to room temperature.

To serve, wait until the terrine is cold, then remove the foil and plastic wrap and slowly invert onto a serving plate, then turn it over so it stands upright. Refrigerate until it is set and serve with cornichons and crusty bread.

CONFIT RABBIT AND POTATO PIE

Makes 4

1 quantity rabbit confit
  (pages 114–115)

PASTRY

400 g (14 oz/2⅔ cups)
  unbleached plain
  (all-purpose) flour

a pinch of salt

2 free-range eggs, beaten

100 g (3½ oz) rendered goose
  or duck fat

100 g (3½ oz) butter, plus
  extra for greasing

To make the pastry, put the flour and salt in a non-reactive bowl and make a well in the centre. Add the egg, stir through and set aside.

Put the goose fat, butter and 200 ml (7 fl oz) water in a saucepan over medium heat and bring it up to melting temperature — do not boil it. Once it has melted, add it to the flour mixture and stir through. Start to knead the pastry until it becomes very silky. Wrap in plastic wrap and refrigerate for at least 1 hour.

Preheat the oven to 170°C (325°F/Gas 3). Lightly grease four 10 cm (4 inch) round loose-based cake or pie tins with a little butter.

Remove the pastry from the refrigerator and divide it into four even-sized portions. Cut a quarter from each portion to make four pie lids. Roll out each portion of pastry to make four circles, each with a 20 cm (8 inch) diameter, about 5 mm (¼ inch) thick and line the base and side of the prepared tins.

Take the meat and vegetables and distribute it between the pies. Roll out the remaining pastry to make lids large enough to cover the pies. Make a hole in the top of each for steam to escape during cooking. Brush a little water over the rim of the lids and pinch the edges to seal, trimming any excess pastry. Cook the pies in the oven for 40 minutes, or until the tops are golden brown. Remove from the oven and set aside for 10–15 minutes before removing from the tins. These pies are best eaten hot but are also great served cold.

CONFIT, RILLETTES, PÂTÉ AND TERRINE

PÂTÉ EN CROÛTE

Makes 1.5 kg (3 lb 5 oz) loaf

*This is the real deal of French charcuterie and such a simple thing to do —
baking a terrine inside some pastry. Or so it seems. But to eat a perfect
pâté en croûte is one of the greatest culinary pleasures you can indulge in.*

To make the jelly, put all of the ingredients into a stockpot or large saucepan with enough water to cover, and bring to the boil. Reduce the heat to low and simmer until the liquid reduces to a syrupy consistency. Remove from the heat and set aside to cool.

To make the pastry, put the butter, flour and salt into a food processor and pulse until the mixture has a sand-like texture (you can do this with your hands in a bowl if you wish). Heat 150 ml (5 fl oz) water to just under boiling point and add this to the pastry, then pulse or stir very quickly so no lumps form. Knead the dough until it is a little bit silky, then cover in plastic wrap and refrigerate for at least 1 hour.

Preheat the oven to 165°C (320°F/Gas 2–3). Set aside one-fifth of the pastry for the lid. Roll out the remaining pastry to make a large rectangle. Gently lower the pastry into a 31 x 8 x 8 cm (12½ x 3¼ x 3¼ inch) rectangular tin to line the base and sides, making sure it is large enough to overhang the sides. »

1 portion terrine (page 119)

PASTRY

175 g (6 oz) chilled butter, chopped

500 g (1 lb 2 oz/3⅓ cups) unbleached plain (all-purpose) flour

10 g (¼ oz) salt

JELLY

4 pig's trotters, ask your butcher to split them in half

1 brown onion, peeled and halved

2 purple garlic cloves

3 fresh thyme sprigs

5 juniper berries

1 bay leaf

170 ml (5½ fl oz/⅔ cup) Marsala

» Press the terrine mixture into the mould over the pastry, making sure there are no air holes. Roll out the reserved pastry to make a rectangle large enough for the lid, then brush the edges with a little water and use your fingers to crimp the pastry at the edges to seal. Cut two flute holes in the top and place a foil chimney in each so the terrine can breath during cooking — this will stop the pastry going soggy. Cook in the oven for 70 minutes, or until the liquid that comes out the top is completely clear. Remove from the oven and allow to cool.

If the jelly has set, slightly reheat it until you can strain the liquid. Let the liquid cool down to room temperature in a jug, as it needs to be pourable. After you take the pastry-enclosed terrine out of the mould, slowly pour the jelly liquid into the chimney holes — do this in stages until it is full, then refrigerate overnight. To serve, simply cut the pâté en croûte into slices and enjoy with good mustard, pickles and crusty bread.

SAUSAGES

A good sausage, despite what you may have heard, eaten or read, is made from good meat. It isn't a hospital, and no meat going into a sausage is going to get better simply by being put in a casing. That said, you can finely mince up some harder-to-use bits to make very good products, but bland, watery, lean factory farmed meat won't ever make a very good banger.

We like to use old-breed meats, particularly pork, for its flavour. Berkshire has a really wonderful porky taste. Wessex Saddlebacks have a luscious sweet flavour and plenty of fat. We also think free-range pigs, which are slower growing, are a cut above. The best result comes if the meat is both from an old breed and free range.

A good sausage, in our view, doesn't have fillers such as rice flour or gluten. It doesn't have binders or emulsifiers, and certainly doesn't have preservatives (though a salami may benefit from some special curing salt). A good sausage tastes of the animal from which it came; meaty, yet more complex than a simple roast; rich with enough fat to make it moist without being greasy; and always delicately seasoned to let the true taste of good-quality meat shine through. The best-flavoured meat for sausages is shoulder — a working muscle that is good minced. Invest in a quality mincer before you start.

TOULOUSE SAUSAGES

Makes about 15–20 sausages

The Toulouse is one of our favourite sausages. It relies on great pork. Old-breeds are best for this sausage as there is no fat added to the minced shoulder. It's just tasty pork with a little bit of technique involved, which highlights the pleasure and simplicity of making your own sausages. Be mindful of the amount of nutmeg you add to flavour these sausages, as too much will create numbness on the palate.

Soak the sausage casing in cold water for 1 hour, then rinse it well inside and out. Thread the casing onto the sausage nozzle, put it onto a plate and keep in the refrigerator.

Remove the sanitised mincer parts from the freezer (see page 134) and assemble the mincer as per the manufacturer's instructions. Cut the meat into pieces small enough to grind through the mincer. Using a medium-sized disc, grind the meat into a non-reactive bowl that has been sanitised and kept in the freezer.

Wash and sanitise your hands (some people prefer to use gloves, but we think you can lose the feel of what you are doing, and with sausage making that is important). Combine the ground meat with the salt, pepper and nutmeg. Place in the refrigerator.

Fill the bowl of the sausage cannon with the mixture — be careful not to leave any air pockets as this will create air pockets in the sausages, which you want to avoid. Attach the nozzle to the end of the sausage cannon. Tie a knot at the end of the casing, pumping the mixture out of the end of the nozzle before »

- **1 full-length natural hog casing**
- **2 kg (4 lb 8 oz) old-breed free-range pork shoulder, skin off (see note)**
- **20 g (¾ oz) pure sea salt**
- **1 tablespoon ground white pepper**
- **1 pinch ground nutmeg**

» you tie the knot as this will also stop air pockets from forming. Slowly start to crank the cannon and fill the casing to make sausages. Be careful not to overfill or underfill the casing — overfill and you will break the casing every time you twist it to form links; underfill it and you will be left with baggy snag bags. It gets much easier with practice.

Guide the casing out of the cannon using your thumb and forefinger onto a clean work surface as it fills. Once it has finished, massage the sausage to ensure that it is filled evenly. From the end that is tied, twist the filled casing at 13 cm (5 inch) intervals to make individual sausages. Once you come to the end, tie the final knot. Hang the sausages overnight in a coolroom or the refrigerator to set (see page 134). Use within a couple of days or wrap tightly in plastic wrap and freeze.

NOTE: *If you haven't got your hands on some old-breed pork with a good ratio of fat to meat (fat would be about 15–20%), you will need to replace some meat with minced pork back fat.*

VARIATION: *You can also make Tuscan pork and fennel sausages by omitting the nutmeg and replacing it with 1 tablespoon ground fennel and 1 tablespoon fennel seeds.*

SAUSAGES

ENGLISH PORK SAUSAGES

Makes about 15–20 sausages

To the English, this sausage is the breakfast staple equivalent of Vegemite to Australians. It is typically a bulk-produced, highly processed product, but once you have had a good English pork sausage then you will know what all the fuss is about.

Soak the sausage casing in cold water for 1 hour, then rinse it well inside and out. Thread the casing onto the sausage nozzle, put it onto a plate and keep in the refrigerator.

Remove the sanitised mincer parts from the freezer (see page 134) and assemble the mincer as per the manufacturer's instructions. Cut the meat into pieces small enough to grind through the mincer. Using a medium-sized disc, grind the meat into a stainless steel bowl that has been sanitised and kept in the freezer.

Wash and sanitise your hands (some people prefer to use gloves, but we think you can lose the feel of what you are doing, and with sausage making that is important). Combine the ground meat, bread, mace, cloves, thyme, salt, pepper and nutmeg. Place it back through the mincer on a fine blade that has been kept in the freezer. Afterwards, mix in »

1 full-length natural hog casing

2 kg (4 lb 8 oz) old-breed, free-range pork shoulder, skin off (see note, page 129)

300 g (10½ oz) fresh white bread slices, pulled apart

1 tablespoon ground mace

1 tablespoon ground cloves

1 tablespoon finely chopped fresh thyme

20 g (¾ oz) pure sea salt

1 tablespoon ground white pepper

1 pinch freshly grated nutmeg

8 free-range egg yolks

» the egg yolks, using your hands to thoroughly combine, or you will fail to get that silken texture. If you have a dough mixer that is big enough, you can mix it that way. Place in the refrigerator.

Fill the bowl of the sausage cannon with the mixture — be careful not to leave any air pockets as this will create air pockets in the sausages, which you want to avoid. Attach the nozzle to the end of the sausage cannon. Tie a knot at the end of the casing, pumping the mixture out of the end of the nozzle before you tie the knot as this will also stop air pockets from forming. Slowly start to crank the cannon and fill the casing to make sausages. Be careful not to overfill or underfill the casing —

overfill and you will break the casing every time you twist it to form links; underfill them and you will be left with baggy snag bags. It gets much easier with practice.

Guide the casing out of the cannon using your thumb and forefinger onto a clean work surface as it fills. Once it has finished, massage the sausage to ensure that it is filled evenly. From the end that is tied, twist the filled casing at 13 cm (5 inch) intervals to make individual sausages. Once you come to the end, tie the final knot. Hang the sausages overnight in a coolroom or the refrigerator to set (see page 134). Use within a couple of days or wrap tightly in plastic wrap and freeze.

BULL-BOAR SAUSAGES

Makes about 15–20 sausages

Bull-boar is a sausage where the name says it all — it is half bull, half boar. Traditionally when making this sausage, they used old retired dairy cows, but you can substitute this for aged beef. It has its origins in the goldfields of central Victoria and was made by the Swiss–Italian border immigrants. They are also one of the five foods of Australia listed in the 'Ark of Taste' by Slow Food. The Ark of Taste aims to preserve and promote unique foods from regions throughout the world that have been sustainably produced. This sausage mix is best refrigerated overnight before you fill the casing.

Soak the sausage casing in cold water for 1 hour, then rinse it well inside and out. Thread the casing onto the sausage nozzle, put it onto a plate and keep in the refrigerator.

Remove the sanitised mincer parts from the freezer (see page 134) and assemble the mincer as per the manufacturer's instructions. Cut the meat into pieces small enough to grind through the mincer. Using a medium-sized disc, grind the meat into a non-reactive bowl that has been sanitised and kept in the freezer.

Wash and sanitise your hands (some people prefer to use gloves, but we think you can lose the feel of what you are doing, and with sausage making that is important). Combine the ground meat with the garlic, spices, wine, salt and pepper. Cover and refrigerate overnight. »

1 full-length natural hog casing

1 kg (2 lb 4 oz) free-range pork shoulder, skin off (see note, page 129)

1 kg (2 lb 4 oz) grass-fed beef topside

8 purple garlic cloves, crushed

1 tablespoon ground mace

1 tablespoon ground cinnamon

1 tablespoon ground pimento

1 tablespoon freshly grated nutmeg

1 tablespoon cayenne pepper

750 ml (26 fl oz/3 cups) full-bodied red wine

20 g (¾ oz) pure sea salt

20 g (¾ oz) freshly ground black pepper

» The next day, fill the bowl of the sausage cannon with the mixture — be careful not to leave any air pockets as this will create air pockets in the sausages, which you want to avoid. Attach the nozzle to the end of the sausage cannon. Tie a knot at the end of the casing, pumping the mixture out of the end of the nozzle before you tie the knot as this will also stop air pockets from forming. Slowly start to crank the cannon and fill the casing to make sausages. Be careful not to overfill or underfill the casing — overfill and you will break the casing every time you twist it to form links; underfill them and you will be left with baggy snag bags.

Guide the casing out of the cannon using your thumb and forefinger onto a clean work surface as it fills. Once it has finished, massage the sausage to ensure that it is filled evenly. From the end that is tied, twist the filled casing at 13 cm (5 inch) intervals to make individual sausages. Once you come to the end, tie the final knot. Hang the sausages overnight in a coolroom or the refrigerator (see page 134). Use within a couple of days or wrap tightly in plastic wrap and freeze.

SAUSAGE MAKING

There are a couple of rules when making your own bangers. Hygiene is one. Keep the meat cool, wash your hands well before and during the making, and sanitise (sterilise) the equipment you use. (A baby sanitiser, available at most supermarkets, works well for domestic sausage making.) Use non-reactive dishes so nothing will rust or oxidise, and keep all your equipment as cold as possible to help the meat emulsify properly — popping the mincer parts into the freezer before using is a great way to do this.

Sausages need to be hung for a day (at least 12 hours) after making or they will not have bound together properly and will split when cooked. And we're huge fans of natural casings (sheep for chipolatas, pork for nice fat sausages and ox casings – or bungs for salami and cotechino). Often they're sold packed in salt, and need soaking for an hour before use. They're the intestines of the animal that have been cleaned well but they do spiral around and need to be untangled before use. Pop the casings over a tap on low and let the cold water find its way through the casings as you untangle them. Some modern casings are sold already untangled and ready to go, pulled over plastic tubing. They're expensive, but an awful lot easier to work with. Never let any type of casings go dry or they will become unmanageable, and watch out for holes, as this will seriously disrupt the pumping of the sausages.

Ideally you'll have or can borrow a sausage cannon to pump out the mince into the casings. If not, a piping (icing) bag may do the trick, but it's slow and painful by comparison.

COTECHINO SAUSAGES

Makes about 4–6 large sausages

The 'cote' in cotechino means skin, and it is simply not cotechino without the skin. This sausage is served poached or fried, but you can only fry it after it has been poached. If fried, the skin inside the casing crisps up like nothing else, but the gelatinous texture you get when poached in a good stock is second to none. It's a hard one to choose — you will have to try it both ways and decide for yourself.

1 full-length natural ox casing

2 kg (4 lb 8 oz) old-breed, free-range pork shoulder, including skin

1 kg (2 lb 4 oz) pork skin

105 g (3½ oz/1 cup) grated pecorino cheese

6 purple garlic cloves, crushed

1 tablespoon ground cinnamon

1 tablespoon cayenne pepper

1 tablespoon ground cloves

1 pinch freshly grated nutmeg

30 g (1 oz) pure sea salt

2 tablespoons freshly ground black pepper

water or stock, for poaching

Soak the sausage casing in cold water for 1 hour, then rinse it well inside and out. Thread the casing onto the sausage nozzle, put it onto a plate and keep in the refrigerator.

Remove the sanitised mincer parts from the freezer (see page 134) and assemble the mincer as per the manufacturer's instructions. Cut the meat and skin into pieces small enough to grind through the mincer, but keep them separate. The skin will be the hardest part to mince and you may need to put it through twice. Using a medium-sized disc, grind the meat and then the skin into a non-reactive bowl that has been sanitised and kept in the freezer.

Wash and sanitise your hands (some people prefer to use gloves, but we think you can lose the feel of what you are doing, and with sausage making that is important). Combine the ground meat and skin, pecorino, garlic, cinnamon, cayenne pepper, cloves, nutmeg, salt and pepper. Make sure you combine all the ingredients thoroughly or you will fail to get a silken texture. If you have a dough mixer that is big enough, you can mix it that way. Place in the refrigerator.

Fill the bowl of the sausage cannon with the mixture — be careful not to leave any air pockets as this will create air pockets in the sausages, which you want to avoid. Attach the nozzle to the end of the sausage cannon. Tie a knot at the end of the casing, pumping the mixture out of the end of the nozzle before you tie the knot as this will also stop air pockets from forming. Slowly start to crank the cannon and fill the casing to make sausages. Make sure when you fill this sausage that it is packed tight as it is easier to make this type of sausage one at a time. Guide the casing out of the cannon using your thumb and forefinger onto a clean work surface as it fills. Once it has finished, massage the sausage to ensure that it is filled evenly. Once it has reached about 30 cm (12 inches) in length, stop and tie the end off. Repeat until all the mixture has been used. Hang the sausage for 3 hours (see page 91).

After the cotechino has hung, place the sausage in simmering water or stock for about 1–2 hours, or until the sausage floats on top of the water. If you want to eat the sausage with stock go right ahead, but if you want to fry it, you will have to refrigerate it overnight to allow it to set. It is then best cooked in slices in a frying pan over high heat for 5 minutes each side — these sausages should crisp up nicely.

BOUDIN BLANC SAUSAGES

Makes about 15–20 sausages

This is the pinnacle of sausage making. If you can make a great boudin blanc then the world is yours. Making an emulsified sausage is hard because they are likely to split if they get too hot, so they won't bind as well, which can change the texture. It takes a bit of skill but the result is incredible flavour. The key to emulsified sausages is keeping everything cold, working in small batches, and working fast.

To make the milk infusion, put all of the ingredients into a saucepan and bring to the boil. Reduce the heat to low and simmer for 10 minutes, then strain and set aside to cool. Discard the vegetables and flavourings.

Soak the sausage casing in cold water for 1 hour, then rinse it well inside and out. Thread the casing onto the sausage nozzle, put it onto a plate and keep in the refrigerator.

Remove the sanitised mincer parts from the freezer (see page 134) and assemble the mincer as per the manufacturer's instructions. Cut the meat and back fat into pieces small enough to grind through the mincer. Using a medium-sized disc, grind the meat into a non-reactive bowl that has been sanitised and kept in the freezer.

Wash and sanitise your hands (some people prefer to use gloves, but we think you can lose the feel of what you are doing, and with sausage making that is important). Combine the ground meat and back fat, salt, white pepper, nutmeg and sugar and mix well. Put the mixture back through the mincer on a fine blade that has been kept in the freezer. Combine the eggs, egg whites, port, cornflour and milk infusion in a jug.   »

1 full-length natural hog casing

1.5 kg (3 lb 5 oz) free-range pork shoulder, skin off (see note, page 129)

500 g (1 lb 2 oz) pork back fat

30 g (1 oz) pure sea salt

10 g (¼ oz) white pepper

a pinch of freshly grated nutmeg

a pinch of sugar

2 free-range eggs

6 free-range egg whites

2 tablespoons port

40 g (1½ oz/⅓ cup) cornflour (cornstarch)

MILK INFUSION

500 ml (17 fl oz/2 cups) full-cream (whole) milk

1 onion, sliced

1 carrot, halved lengthways

2 bay leaves

5 fresh thyme sprigs

½ vanilla bean, split lengthways

10 g (¼ oz) dried porcini (cep) mushrooms

» Working in small batches, combine some of the meat and liquid in a food processor and pulse to combine, being very careful not to overwork it. Make sure you place the combined mixture into the refrigerator once combined and repeat until all of the mixture is processed and refrigerated.

Fill the bowl of the sausage cannon with the mixture — be careful not to leave any air pockets as this will create air pockets in the sausages, which you want to avoid. Attach the nozzle to the end of the sausage cannon. Tie a knot at the end of the casing, pumping the mixture out of the end of the nozzle before you tie the knot as this will also stop air pockets from forming. Slowly start to crank the cannon and fill the casing to make sausages. Be careful not to overfill or underfill the casing — overfill and you will break the casing every time you twist it to form links; underfill them and you will be left with baggy snag bags. Guide the casing out of the cannon using your thumb and forefinger onto a clean work surface as it fills. Once it has finished, massage the sausage to ensure that it is filled evenly. From the end that is tied, twist the filled casing at 13 cm (5 inch) intervals to make individual sausages. Once you come to the end, tie the final knot. Hang for 3 hours (see page 91) — place a tray or similar below to catch any liquid that drains from the sausages.

Fill a large saucepan with water and bring to the boil. Add the sausages, return to a boil, then reduce the heat to low and poach the sausages for about 10–15 minutes, or until they float. Remove the sausages and transfer them immediately to an ice bath. Once cool, pat them dry with kitchen paper and refrigerate. To serve the sausages you can lightly pan-fry them or reheat in a little stock.

FRANKFURTER SAUSAGES

Makes about 20–25

Who hasn't had frankfurters? It's a sausage that has been destroyed by many over the years. This recipe is based more on a Knackwurst sausage and will hopefully restore your faith in the humble hot dog.

Follow the first two preparatory steps in the method for Toulouse sausages (page 128–129).

Wash and sanitise your hands (some people prefer to use gloves, but we think you can lose the feel of what you are doing, and with sausage making that is important). Combine the ground meat with the salt, pepper, coriander, allspice, mace and garlic and mix very well. Place it back through the mincer on a fine blade. Refrigerate.

Fill the bowl of the sausage cannon with the mixture — be careful not to leave any air pockets. Attach the nozzle to the end of the sausage cannon. Tie a knot at the end of the casing, pumping the mixture out of the end of the nozzle before you tie the knot. Slowly start to crank the cannon and fill the casing to make sausages. Make sure when you fill this sausage that it is packed tight. Guide the casing out of the cannon using your thumb and forefinger onto a clean work surface as it fills. Once it has finished, massage the sausage to ensure that it is filled evenly. From the end that is tied, twist the filled casing at 13 cm (5 inch) intervals to make individual sausages. Once you come to the end, tie the final knot. Hang for 3 hours (see page 91).

Place the sausages in a smoker and hot smoke them at 75°C (167°F) for 25–30 minutes. They are best eaten straight out of the smoker. If you have any leftovers they do freeze well.

2 full lengths natural sheep casing

1 kg (2 lb 4 oz) free-range pork shoulder, skin off (see note, page 129)

1 kg (2 lb 4 oz) grass-fed veal shoulder

20 g (¾ oz) pure sea salt

1 tablespoon freshly ground black pepper

1 tablespoon ground coriander

1 tablespoon ground allspice

1 tablespoon ground mace

7 purple garlic cloves, crushed

CEVAPCICI SAUSAGES

Makes about 40

This is a sausage I am surprised hasn't taken over in popularity from the ubiquitous 'bbq' sausage in Australia. It has all the elements you need — it tastes great, it's best cooked on a barbecue and it is quick and easy to make as it is skinless. It has its origins in the Balkans in south-east Europe, which also has a strong affiliation with Australia. If you are in a hurry, get your butcher to mince the meat for you, then it's just a 15-minute job.

750 g (1 lb 10 oz) free-range pork shoulder, skin off (see note, page 129)

500 g (1 lb 2 oz) lean, grass-fed beef

250 g (9 oz) lamb

1 free-range egg white

4 purple garlic cloves, crushed

15 g (½ oz) pure sea salt

1 teaspoon bicarbonate of soda (baking soda)

2 teaspoons freshly ground black pepper

½ teaspoon cayenne pepper

1 teaspoon sweet paprika

Remove the sanitised mincer parts from the freezer (see page 134) and assemble the mincer as per the manufacturer's instructions. Cut the meat into pieces small enough to grind through the mincer. Using a medium-sized disc, grind the meat into a non-reactive bowl that has been sanitised and kept in the freezer.

Wash and sanitise your hands (some people prefer to use gloves, but we think you can lose the feel of what you are doing, and with sausage making that is important). Combine all of the ingredients until it forms a paste-like texture.

Using a clean piping (icing) bag without a nozzle attachment, fill with the meat mixture and slowly push the mixture out the end to make sausages about 7–9 cm (2¾–3½ inches) long. Alternatively, you could use a sausage cannon. These sausages are ready to cook straight away — they will need about 5–7 minutes on each side. They also freeze really well.

BANGERS AND MASH WITH ONION GRAVY

Serves 4

The best way to cook the onions is in the sausage pan, so you'll need to either get them started in the pan before frying the bangers, or use a big pan and do them all at once. Just be sure to remove the sausages before adding the flour.

1 kg (2 lb 4 oz) starchy potatoes, peeled

2 teaspoons lard

4 brown onions, thinly sliced

2 fresh thyme sprigs

8 fat pork sausages, such as Toulouse (pages 128-129)

1 tablespoon plain (all-purpose) flour

2 tablespoons red wine

a splash of worcestershire sauce or a dab of beef jelly from underneath some dripping if you have it, or even a tiny nugget of Vegemite to bring up the flavour

200 g (7 oz) cultured butter, cut into small cubes (pages 12–13)

100 ml (3½ fl oz) full-cream (whole) milk, heated

Put the potatoes on to steam or boil and get the bangers on. Heat the lard in a large frying pan over medium heat and gently fry the onions with the thyme until they soften and start to colour. It's best if you stir them often as they cook. You can fish them out at this point and fry the bangers in the same pan. Remove the sausages and keep them warm in the oven while you finish making the gravy.

Return the onion to the pan and stir in the flour, keeping the pan over medium heat. You want the flour to cook out a little, but not really darken. If the flour is way too crumbly, you may need to add a touch of fat, but there should be plenty from the lard and snags. Tip in the red wine and continue to stir well as it boils and thickens into the flour. Add 300 ml (10½ fl oz) water (you can use the steaming water from any vegetables) a little at a time, stirring well after each addition, to make a thick but not gluggy gravy. Add the worcestershire or other flavouring and taste for salt and pepper. Remove from the heat and keep warm.

Mash the potatoes with the butter and milk until smooth and season well. Serve with the sausages and the onion gravy over the top.

THE WORLD'S BEST HOT DOG

Serves 4

It might have its roots in New York and Chicago but the hot dog has definitely become global and accordingly, everyone has become an expert on what makes the definitive hot dog. Well, here is the right answer!

In a small bowl, mix the dill pickle and white onion and set aside. Cut the rolls lengthways and spread with the mustard.

Heat the sunflower oil in a frying pan over medium heat and fry the brown onion until soft and golden brown, about 8 minutes. Remove from the pan and set aside. Make five small cuts on one side of each frankfurter, then add them to the same pan and fry them for 3 minutes on each side, or until they are heated through.

Place a frankfurter in each roll. Press any excess liquid out of the sauerkraut using kitchen paper, then add to the hot dog. Sprinkle the cooked onion and the pickle mixture over the top, then add tomato sauce and celery salt according to how you like it.

2 dill pickles (page 220), finely diced

1 small white onion, finely diced

4 long crusty bread rolls

Ross's wholegrain mustard (page 248)

1 tablespoon sunflower oil

1 large brown onion, thinly sliced

4 frankfurters (page 140)

100 g (3½ oz) sauerkraut (page 227)

Grandpa Steve's tomato sauce (ketchup) (page 242)

celery salt

CEVAPCICI, POTATO, FRESH HERB AND RED ONION SALAD WITH CRÈME FRAÎCHE

Serves 6

1 kg (2 lb 4 oz) pink-eye potatoes, washed with skin on

1 red onion, thinly sliced

1 bunch fresh flat-leaf (Italian) parsley, leaves picked

1 bunch fresh coriander (cilantro), leaves picked

1 bunch fresh chives, snipped

300 g (10½ oz) crème fraîche (page 9)

18–24 cevapcici sausages, (page 141)

olive oil, for drizzling

a pinch of sweet paprika

Cook the potatoes in a saucepan of salted boiling water for 10–15 minutes, or until tender, then drain and leave to cool.

Put the onion, parsley, coriander and chives in a serving bowl. Cut the warm potatoes and add to the bowl with 200 g (7 oz) of the crème fraîche. Season well with sea salt and freshly ground black pepper and stir into the salad. Set aside.

Heat a barbecue grill plate to medium — wood or coal fuelled is preferable, as this will add a better flavour to the meat when cooking. Drizzle the cevapcici with a little olive oil and cook the cevapcici for 5–7 minutes, turning as needed until they are evenly coloured — they will be firm in texture when done.

When the cevapcici are cooked, arrange over the salad and sprinkle the paprika on top. Serve the remaining crème fraîche on the side.

BOUDIN BLANC WITH BARLEY AND PUMPKIN

Serves 4

Pearl barley makes a beautiful 'risotto', adding a nuttiness and texture that is missing in the rice versions. This is very much a winter dish, comforting like 'bangers and mash' but just a bit more highbrow.

Preheat the oven to 180°C (350°F/Gas 4). In a roasting tin, put the pumpkin, thyme, rosemary, garlic cloves and walnut oil, season with sea salt and freshly ground black pepper, and toss together so that all the pumpkin is coated in oil and well seasoned. Roast for 30 minutes, or until golden and softened. Use the back of a wooden spoon to partly smash up the pumpkin and set aside.

Heat the extra virgin olive oil in a large heavy-based frying pan over medium heat and sauté the onion for 5 minutes, or until soft. Add the pearl barley and bay leaves and stir for 1 minute to coat, then add the stock. Bring to the boil, then reduce the heat to low and simmer for about 30 minutes, stirring occasionally until the barley is soft — you may need to add a little water if it looks a bit dry.

Meanwhile, heat a little olive oil in a frying pan over medium heat. Add the boudin blanc and cook until golden brown and warmed through. Cover and keep warm.

Add the pumpkin to the barley in the pan and stir through. Cook for a further 1 minute. Place a ladleful of the risotto on each serving plate. Sprinkle with the parsley and drizzle over a little extra walnut oil. Place the warm boudin blanc on top of the barley to serve.

500 g (1 lb 2 oz) pumpkin (winter squash), peeled, seeded and cut into small cubes

1 teaspoon chopped fresh thyme

1 teaspoon chopped fresh rosemary

8 purple garlic cloves, peeled

2 tablespoons walnut oil, plus extra, for drizzling

1 tablespoon extra virgin olive oil

1 brown onion, finely diced

300 g (10½ oz/1½ cups) pearl barley

3 bay leaves

1 litre (35 fl oz/4 cups) chicken stock

olive oil, for frying

8 poached boudin blanc sausages (pages 138–139)

2 tablespoons finely chopped fresh flat-leaf (Italian) parsley

COTECHINO, SHREDDED PORK BROTH AND POTATO DUMPLINGS

Serves 6

1 kg (2 lb 4 oz) pork bones

1 white onion, peeled and cut into quarters

2 purple garlic bulbs, cut in half widthways

1 leek, roughly chopped

1 celery stalk, roughly chopped

2 carrots, halved lengthways

2 bay leaves

5 juniper berries

½ bunch fresh thyme

1 raw cotechino sausage (pages 136–137)

500 g (1 lb 2 oz) old-breed, free-range boneless pork shoulder

2 handfuls fresh flat-leaf (Italian) parsley, chopped

POTATO DUMPLINGS

500 g (1 lb 2 oz) whole waxy potatoes, such as King Edwards or Dutch creams, washed with skin on

100 g (3½ oz/⅔ cup) plain (all-purpose) flour

1 free-range egg

1 bunch chives, finely snipped

a pinch each of salt, freshly ground black pepper and freshly grated nutmeg

Preheat the oven to 250°C (500°F/Gas 9). Roast the pork bones in a roasting tin until they are golden brown, about 35 minutes. Transfer the bones to a stockpot or large saucepan. Put the onion, garlic, leek, celery, carrot, bay leaves, juniper berries and thyme into the same roasting tin and return to the oven for 15 minutes, then add to the pot. Deglaze the tin with a little water and add it to the pot.

Place the sausage and the pork shoulder into the stockpot and add enough water to cover. Bring to the boil, then reduce the heat and simmer, uncovered, for 3–4 hours. If the sausage and shoulder are floating, turn them a couple of times to ensure they cook evenly. Remove the cotechino and pork shoulder and set aside. Strain the stock, discarding the vegetables; skim the fat from the surface. Slice the cotechino and shred the pork shoulder and place into a serving bowl.

To make the dumplings, cook the potatoes in a saucepan of salted boiling water. Drain well, then pass through a mouli into a non-reactive bowl. Set aside to cool. Combine the potato with the flour, egg, chives, salt, pepper and nutmeg. Roll one-quarter of the potato mixture at a time into a long cylinder with a diameter of about 3 cm (1¼ inches). Make a cut every 1.5 cm (⅝ inch) and roll into balls.

Heat the reserved stock in a saucepan, add the dumplings and simmer for 2 minutes, or until they float. Add the parsley and pour the stock and dumplings over the cotechino and pork. Great served on a winter's night.

SALUMI

Dried or fermented sausages are products that are very close to our hearts. It's amazing how such a simple product can drive so much flavour and texture. The three smallgoods included in this section — chorizo, saucisson sec and coppa — are a great cross-section of European varieties, of which there are many to choose from. We think these ones stand out from the rest.

CHORIZO

Makes about 7–9

Chorizo is a sausage that you can eat at three different stages. The first is fresh and cooked on a barbecue as normal; the second is hung and cured for a couple of weeks and then sliced and fried and eaten inside fresh bread. The last is to let it hang for 4 weeks until it is hard, like a good salami. Try the different stages and see which is best for you.

Soak the sausage casing in cold water for 1 hour, then rinse it well inside and out. Thread the casing onto the sausage nozzle, put it onto a plate and keep in the refrigerator.

Remove the sanitised mincer parts from the freezer (see page 134) and assemble the mincer as per the manufacturer's instructions. Cut the meat into pieces small enough to grind through the mincer. Using a medium-sized disc, grind the meat into a non-reactive bowl that has been sanitised and kept in the freezer.

Wash and sanitise your hands (some people prefer to use gloves, but we think you can lose the feel of what you are doing, and with sausage making that is important). Combine the ground meat with the garlic, spices, wine, salt, pepper, starter culture and sodium nitrate, if using, and mix very well. Place in the refrigerator and leave overnight.

The next day, fill the bowl of the sausage cannon with the mixture — be careful not to leave any air pockets as this will create air pockets in the chorizo, which you want to avoid. Attach the nozzle to the end of the sausage cannon. Tie a knot at the end of the   »

1 full-length natural hog casing

2 kg (4 lb 8 oz) free-range pork shoulder, skin off (see note, page 129)

7 purple garlic cloves, crushed

2 tablespoons smoked paprika

2 tablespoons sweet paprika

1 tablespoon dried oregano

1 tablespoon ground cumin

1 teaspoon dried chilli flakes

300 ml (10½ fl oz) red wine

40 g (1½ oz) pure sea salt

20 g (¾ oz) freshly ground black pepper

a pinch of starter culture (see note)

a pinch of sodium nitrate (optional) (see note, page 90)

» casing, pumping the mixture out of the end of the nozzle before you tie the knot as this will also stop air pockets from forming. Slowly start to crank the cannon and fill the casing to make the chorizo. Make sure when you fill the casing that it is packed tight.

Guide the casing out of the cannon using your thumb and forefinger onto a clean work surface as it fills. Once it has finished, massage the sausage to ensure that it is filled evenly. From the end that is tied, twist the filled casing at 23 cm (9 inch) intervals to make individual sausages. Once you come to the end, tie the final knot.

Hang the sausages in a cool well-ventilated place, about 17°C (63°F) (see page 91 for notes on hanging). It takes about 2–3 weeks for the sausages to start to dry out — the longer you leave them the drier they will get. We prefer to cook them when they are at the early stage of the drying process.

NOTE: *Starter cultures help to ferment sausages, which in turn develops their colour and flavour and ensures they are safe to eat. For cheese and salami making, it's best to get a commercial starter culture to be sure the right fermentation is happening in the milk or meat. Starter cultures are a good bacteria that give great flavour to a product that could otherwise go off. You can get starter cultures for meats from any butcher's supply stores, there are many to choose from.*

SAUCISSON SEC

Makes about 7–9

Saucisson sec simply means 'dried sausage' in French, so there are many, many recipes for saucisson sec in the same way there are many types of salami — this is the way Ross likes to make his.

Follow the first two preparatory steps in the method for chorizo (see page 156).

Wash and sanitise your hands (some people prefer to use gloves, but we think you can lose the feel of what you are doing, and with sausage making that is important). Combine the ground meat with the garlic, salt, pepper, starter culture and sodium nitrate, if using, and mix very well. Place in the refrigerator.

Fill the bowl of the sausage cannon with the mixture — be careful not to leave any air pockets as this will create air pockets in the sausages. Attach the nozzle to the end of the sausage cannon. Tie a knot at the end of the casing, pumping the mixture out of the end of the nozzle before you tie the knot. Slowly start to crank the cannon and fill the casing to make sausages. Make sure when you fill this sausage that it is packed tight.

Guide the casing out of the cannon using your thumb and forefinger onto a clean work surface as it fills. Once it has finished, massage the sausage to ensure that it is filled evenly. From the end that is tied, twist the filled casing at 23 cm (9 inch) intervals to make individual sausages. Once you come to the end, tie the final knot. Hang the sausages in a cool well-ventilated place, about 17°C (63°F) (see page 91 for notes on hanging). It takes 2–3 weeks for the sausages to start to dry out — the longer you leave them the drier they will get. This sausage is best at about 5 weeks.

1 full-length natural hog casing

2 kg (4 lb 8 oz) free-range pork shoulder, skin off (see note, page 129)

1 purple garlic bulb, cloves peeled and crushed

40 g (1½ oz) pure sea salt

40 g (1½ oz) freshly ground black pepper

a pinch of starter culture (see note, page 157)

a pinch of sodium nitrate (optional) (see note, page 90)

CAPOCOLLO (COPPA)

Makes about 4–6

Which name is it? It's an age-old debate between north and south. Any Italian will tell you there are major differences, but Coppa comes from Piacentina and translates to 'nape' in Italian, referring to the back of the neck, while capocollo comes from Calabria and means 'head', referring to the neck of the pig. So there is a difference, but they taste and look the same.

2 kg (4 lb 8 oz) free-range pork neck, skin off

1 teaspoon ground cloves

1 teaspoon ground cinnamon

1 tablespoon ground juniper berries

1½ tablespoons ground fennel seeds

70 g (2½ oz) pure sea salt

20 g (¾ oz) ground white pepper

a pinch of starter culture (see note, page 157)

a pinch of sodium nitrate (optional) (see note, page 90)

1 full-length natural ox casing

butcher's twine

Cut the pork neck by hand into 5 cm (2 inch) chunks and place into a plastic tub with a lid (zip-lock bags can also be used for this). Add all of the ground spices, salt, pepper, starter culture and sodium nitrate, if using, and mix well. Cover and refrigerate for 2 weeks, turning every couple of days. The meat will be ready when it is firm to touch, as if the muscles are all stiff — if it takes longer, then so be it.

When you are ready to start filling the casing, soak the sausage casing in cold water for 1 hour, then rinse it well inside and out. It is best to tackle these sausages one at a time, as the mixture is quite chunky and you will need to pack them by hand.

Use butcher's twine to tie a knot at one end of the ox casing and cut a length about 30 cm (12 inches) long. Open the top and by hand, pack the meat mixture into the casing as tightly as you can. Once you have finished, tie the other end with twine to secure. If there are still some air pockets, prick these with a sterilised pin and they will dry out in time. Repeat with the remaining casing and meat mixture until all the mixture is used.

Hang the sausages in a cool well-ventilated place, about 17°C (63°F), for about 7–9 weeks before eating (see page 91 for notes on hanging).

SALUMI

BRAISED SQUID STUFFED WITH CHORIZO AND GARLIC WITH CHERRY TOMATOES

Serves 4

90 g (3¼ oz/1½ cups) fresh
sourdough breadcrumbs

1 teaspoon pure sea salt

½ teaspoon freshly ground
black pepper

1 small red chilli, seeded and
finely chopped

1 red onion, finely chopped

1 teaspoon finely grated
lemon zest

1 tablespoon finely chopped
fresh oregano

2 tablespoons chopped fresh
flat-leaf (Italian) parsley

8 purple garlic cloves, peeled
and cut into quarters

1½ teaspoons smoked paprika

1 free-range egg, beaten

2 fresh chorizo sausages (pages
156–157), cut into cubes

6 squid tubes, cleaned and
washed

150 ml (5 fl oz) extra virgin
olive oil

1 red capsicum (pepper),
seeded and sliced into strips

400 g (14 oz) fresh or tinned
cherry tomatoes

1 tablespoon capers, rinsed
and drained

200 ml (7 fl oz) white wine

1 tablespoon sherry vinegar

Preheat the oven to 200°C (400°F/Gas 6).

In a bowl, place the breadcrumbs, salt, pepper, chilli, onion, lemon zest, oregano, parsley, garlic, paprika, egg and chorizo and combine well.

Using your fingers, stuff each squid tube with the mixture until it is almost full. Use a wooden toothpick or skewer to secure the ends of each squid tube.

Heat 1 tablespoon of the olive oil in a frying pan over medium heat. Cook the squid tubes for 2 minutes on each side, or until browned.

Transfer the squid tubes to a baking dish and scatter the capsicum, cherry tomatoes and capers around the squid. Pour over the wine, vinegar and remaining olive oil and bake for 30–40 minutes, or until the squid has turned white, then insert a skewer to check the stuffing is cooked and hot. Cover loosely with foil if the squid is drying out on top and baste with some of the sauce. Serve hot.

PEAS AND BROAD BEANS WITH CAPOCOLLO, BAY LEAVES AND SAFFRON

Serves 4

Fresh peas are a joy. Almost as much as fresh broad (fava) beans. Put them together and you get something that is greater than the sum of its parts. Toss in some cured pork and you take it to another level entirely.

Heat the wine in a small saucepan and add the saffron. Remove from the heat and set aside to bring out the colour and flavour.

Blanch the broad beans in a saucepan of boiling water for about 2 minutes, then drain the beans and refresh them immediately in cold water. Use your fingernail to slit the skin on each bean and then pop out the bright green beans.

Heat the olive oil in a frying pan over medium heat and sauté the onion and garlic for 1–2 minutes, then add the peas, broad beans, bay leaves, stock and wine. Bring to a simmer and cook until the liquid has almost completely reduced. Stir in the sliced capocollo and cook for a further 1 minute.

Remove the pan from the heat, stir in the parsley and season with salt and freshly ground black pepper before serving.

100 ml (3½ fl oz) dry white wine

a pinch of saffron threads

200 g (7 oz) podded broad (fava) beans, from about 800 g (1 lb 12 oz) whole beans

2 tablespoons extra virgin olive oil

1 brown onion, finely diced

1 purple garlic clove, crushed

250 g (9 oz/1⅔ cups) fresh or frozen peas

8 bay leaves

150 ml (5 fl oz) chicken stock

200 g (7 oz) capocollo (coppa) (page 159), sliced into thin strips

3 tablespoons chopped fresh flat-leaf (Italian) parsley

FISH

WHEN DEALING WITH FRESH SEAFOOD, THE EMPHASIS IS ON FRESH. FOR MUCH OF THE WORLD, IF FISH ISN'T FROM THE SAME OR PREVIOUS DAY'S CATCH, IT'S NOT CONSIDERED FRESH. SO, OVER TIME, HUMANITY HAS COME UP WITH MYRIAD WAYS OF PRESERVING FISH AND SHELLFISH TO KEEP IT TASTING GOOD EVEN WHEN IT'S A LONG TIME OUT OF THE WATER.

The recipes in this chapter are for surplus, generally. Instead of freezing fish when you catch a lot, or if you buy it cheap, try creating a whole new range of flavours in the cupboard. Once you've salted your own anchovies, you'll never look at those cheap ones on top of a pizza the same way again. Once you've created a lunch of pickled fish using simple, age-old methods perfected in cooler climes, you'll feel like you've taken a Scandinavian lover. Keep a fillet of fish back to make salt cod and you'll open a whole world of possibilities in terms of flavours — all of these just an arm's length away in your cupboard.

Most seafood can be preserved in some way. Brines, vinegar and salt work well alone or in combination, but think of oily stronger-flavoured fish benefiting from the inclusion of vinegar, and milder fish needing minimal intervention. Of course, you can always add strong flavours later, as we usually would in the case of sardines.

Just as with all preserved foods, there are different methods for yielding different results. For example, fish can be packed in salt, soaked or marinated in an acidic liquid (such as vinegar), smoked or even exposed to heat. Apply any of these methods, or employ a combination, and you not only keep fish for longer, you can make dishes far different from those using the fresh product.

SMOKED FISH

Before you even think of smoking fish, be sure the fish is very fresh, well gutted and scaled, and washed well inside and out — you need to prepare it pretty much the same as if you're cooking it. Then decide whether you want fillets or whole fish. Most of this will depend on how big the fish is, what size smoker you're using, and the type of smoke and flavour you're after (see pages 70–71 for more details on smoking).

All fish for smoking should be salted first. Smoke in isolation isn't as good as smoke and salt together. For most smoked fish we think a brine solution works best, keeping moisture in the meat and curing more delicately than a hard cure using dry salt. If you're in a hurry, as we were once when smoking eel on a riverbank halfway through a canoe trip, you can cure small pieces more quickly with coarse salt or use a salt and sugar mix.

The best brines for fish are made with about 10 per cent salt. That means you would dissolve about 100 g (3½ oz) salt in every 1 litre (35 fl oz/4 cups) water — the amount of brine used will depend on the size of the fish as it will need to be completely immersed. This brine can cure fish fillets or small whole fish in a few hours, or overnight for larger fish or fatter fillets.

SMOKED TUNA

Makes 2 x 375 g (13 oz) pieces

You could use a simple salt and water brine for curing tuna, or any fish for that matter, but for an oily fish like tuna, a few other flavourings can bring out the richness yet cut through the fishy taste. Ginger and bay leaves are two favourites. This recipe suits most fish, but particularly bolder flavoured varieties.

Combine 2.5 litres (87 fl oz) water with the salt, peppercorns, bay leaves, ginger and soy sauce in a large saucepan and bring to the boil. Reduce the heat to low and simmer for 10 minutes, then remove from the heat and allow to cool completely.

Add the tuna to the brine. Leave overnight in the refrigerator before rinsing and cold smoking (see pages 70–71).

Smoke the fish for about 8 hours at a very low temperature, ideally about 20°C (68°F) over a smoker using a sweeter wood, such as apple or cherry.

PER 1 KG (2 LB 4 OZ) MEAT

250 g (9 oz/about 2 cups) pure sea salt

10 whole black peppercorns

2 fresh bay leaves

5 cm (2 inch) piece fresh ginger, hit with a hammer or similar to bruise it

80 ml (2½ fl oz/⅓ cup) soy sauce

2 x 450 g (1 lb) long rectangular pieces of fresh tuna fillet

SMOKED WHOLE TROUT

Serves 2

To prepare smoked trout you need to adjust the brine amounts below to suit the weight of the fish. We have based it on 1 kg (2 lb 4 oz) of fish meat for simplicity. This works well with most oily fish, such as tuna, salmon and trout, but you could use other fish too, taking care not to smoke it so long that it dries out.

Mix together 2.5 litres (87 fl oz) water with the salt, sugar and lemon slices, heating the water if necessary to dissolve the salt and sugar, then cooling before using. Add the whole trout to the brine and leave to soak for about 4 hours.

Drain well, pat the fish dry, then lightly oil and gently hot smoke the trout for about 4 hours at 100°C (200°F), perhaps using a local hardwood such as mountain ash or even sawdust (see pages 70–71).

Hot smoked trout makes a terrific meal tossed through a salad, simply served with buttered potatoes and a little dill mayonnaise, or even flaked through a pasta sauce with a vague hint of cream.

PER 1 KG (2 LB 4 OZ) MEAT

250 g (9 oz/about 2 cups) pure sea salt

1 tablespoon soft brown sugar

2 fresh lemon slices

2 x 500 g (1 lb 2 oz) whole trout, cleaned, scaled and rinsed

SMOKED EEL

Makes 600 g (1 lb 5 oz)

The nature of eel, with its resilient flesh, means that it is conducive to hard curing, that is, curing with salt or a combination of salt and sugar and not with a brine, like many other fish.

PER 1 KG (2 LB 4 OZ) MEAT

80 g (2¾ oz) pure sea salt

55 g (2 oz/¼ cup) caster (superfine) sugar

2½ tablespoons soy sauce

1 kg (2 lb 4 oz) eel

Mix together the salt, sugar and soy sauce and pour two-thirds of the curing mixture into a bowl, reserving the rest to baste the meat while it smokes. Cut the eel into chunks, about 5 cm (2 inches) long, and toss into the bowl. Leave to soak for 1 hour, stirring occasionally, before rinsing and smoking.

Smoke the eel for about 1 hour at about 100°C (200°F) in a smoker, using hickory or vine cuttings (see pages 70–71). Brush with the remaining curing mixture as it cooks so it becomes salty and sticky on the skin. Eat warm or at room temperature.

Smoked eel keeps well in the refrigerator for a week after smoking. Ideally you can serve the eel on steamed rice, as part of a cold meal with rye bread and pickled onions (see page 219), or tossed with dill over hot boiled pink-eye potatoes.

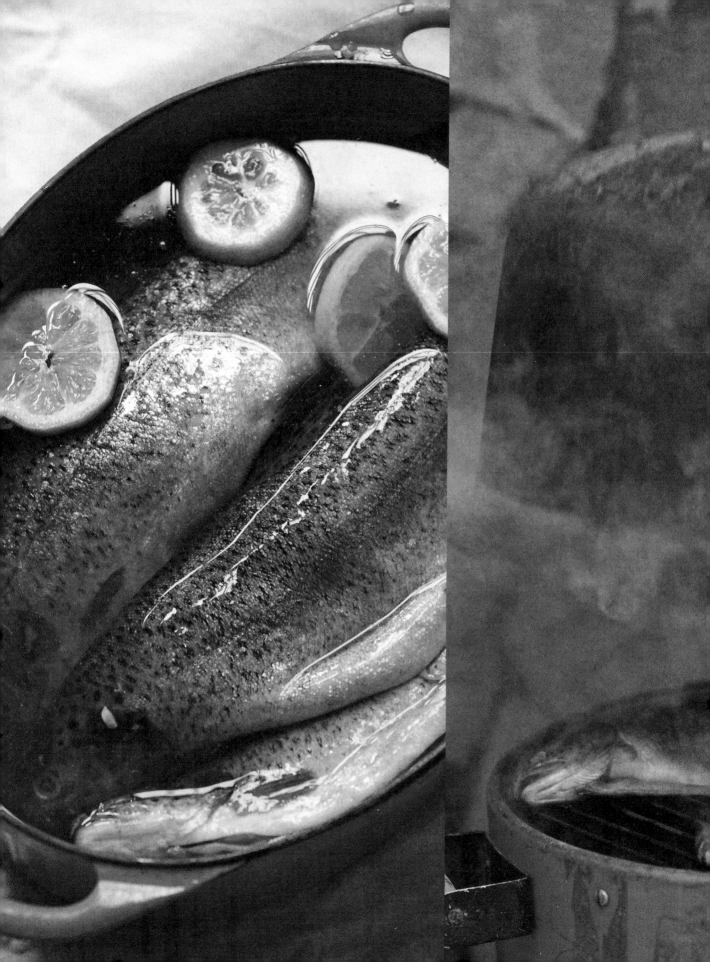

SMOKED TROUT WITH SCRAMBLED EGGS

Serves 2

The creaminess of scrambled eggs with the sharp flavour of smoky fish is so simple, yet so good. Because we have access to farm-fresh eggs, it takes this pairing to another, better, dimension.

1 smoked whole trout
  (page 174)

5 free-range eggs

20 g (¾ oz) butter

1 teaspoon olive oil

4 slices toast, buttered

1 tablespoon snipped fresh
  chives

Remove and discard the skin from the trout and separate the two fillets from the bone. Set aside until it comes to room temperature.

In a non-reactive bowl, crack the eggs and beat with a fork until well combined.

Heat the butter and olive oil in a frying pan over medium heat. Add the egg and when it starts to set on the edges use an egg flip or a wooden spoon to push the mixture in from the side of the pan towards the centre. Continue to tip the egg into the middle in this way until it starts to set evenly all over, being sure to keep the egg moist as it will continue to cook once removed from the heat.

Season the egg with sea salt and freshly ground black pepper, to taste. Divide into two portions and serve over the toast and trout with the chives scattered over the top.

SMOKED TUNA, POTATO AND OLIVE SALAD

Serves 4

There is probably nothing the world needs less than another interpretation of the classic niçoise salad … except if it's one where you have smoked your own tuna, pickled your own olives and made the dressing from scratch. Keep it simple and let the quality of your homemade ingredients speak for themselves.

Put the potatoes into a large saucepan, cover with cold water and add the salt. Bring to the boil over medium–high heat, then reduce the heat to medium and cook for 15–17 minutes, or until tender. Add the beans for the last 3 minutes at the end of cooking. Drain the vegetables and rinse immediately in cold water. When cool enough to handle, cut the potatoes into thick slices.

Put the potato and beans in a large bowl. Add the smoked tuna, tomato, olives and basil leaves. Just before serving, pour over the vinaigrette, season with salt and freshly ground black pepper and toss to combine.

500 g (1 lb 2 oz) waxy potatoes, such as kipfler or pink fir apple, washed with skin on

1 teaspoon pure sea salt

200 g (7 oz) green beans

400 g (14 oz) smoked tuna (page 172), sliced

200 g (7 oz) ripe tomatoes, sliced

100 g (3½ oz) pickled olives (page 228)

1 handful fresh basil leaves

100 ml (3½ fl oz) Matthew's vinaigrette dressing (page 257)

SALT-CURED FISH

It is easy to dismiss the brilliance of salt. While it certainly plays a role in modern kitchens, used mostly as a seasoning to add flavour, its use is but a shadow of its glorious past. Salt has become innocuous, sitting among the random jars and bottles in the pantry, but this common chemical compound made up of sodium and chloride has a long history — it has played a key role in the development of civilisations and global exploration by allowing humans to preserve food that could be consumed months after it was killed or grown. The history of salt-cured fish is almost a parallel story to the history of the world.

We hear a lot about how bad salt is for us but without it, the human body would die; our organs and muscles would fail. At a cellular level, salt regulates the flow and exchange of fluids, principally water. The same chemistry takes place when salt is used to cure food — it sucks water from the cells. Fish is particularly susceptible to spoilage because its flesh has a high water content, which also makes it perfect for salt curing.

Preserving your own fish is a simple process requiring only a few ingredients, so use the best wherever possible: super fresh fish, pure sea salt and extra virgin olive oil. The resulting flavours will turn you off the commercial stuff forever.

SALT-CURED ANCHOVIES

Makes about 500 g (1 lb 2 oz)

You can use sardines or pilchards in this recipe, which are more commonly caught in the waters around Australia. The main difference between curing anchovies and sardines is that anchovies are salt-cured, whereas sardines are salted and cooked in their jars (see opposite).

To remove the fillets from the fish, scrape the back of a spoon along the length of the spine (kind of like scooping them out), starting just behind the gills; discard the heads and bones. This is easier for smaller fish. If the anchovies are big, use a sharp filleting knife.

Place the fillets in a bowl and sprinkle over about 100 g (3½ oz/¾ cup) of the salt and toss to coat. Leave for 10 minutes — this gets rid of any sliminess.

Rinse the fillets in fresh water and pat dry using kitchen paper. Arrange the fillets in layers in a clean plastic container with a lid, sprinkling the remaining salt over each layer until all of the fillets are covered with salt. Seal the container and refrigerate for 1 month.

Pour off the liquid — this liquid can be kept and used as a simple fresh fish sauce with a pronounced fishy taste.

Pack the anchovies into sterilised glass jars (see page 4), pour the olive oil over to cover the anchovies and seal with a tight-fitting lid. Give them a few days to develop their flavour before eating them. We love them tossed through hot pasta with some sambal and good olive oil or finely sliced over super-ripe tomatoes with fresh basil on chargrilled sourdough.

1 kg (2 lb 4 oz) fresh whole anchovies, pilchards or sardines, about 10–15 cm (4–6 inches) long (if using pilchards or anchovies, use smaller fish and make sure they have not been frozen)

500 g (1 lb 2 oz) pure sea salt

500 ml (17 fl oz/2 cups) extra virgin olive oil

SALT-CURED SARDINES

Makes about 500 g (1 lb 2 oz)

If the fish you are starting with are on the big side (over 15 cm/6 inches) you will need to scale them and remove the large back fins. You don't need to fillet or skin the sardines unless they are really big. Make sure that you clean the inside cavity of the fish after you have removed the head and guts.

1 kg (2 lb 4 oz) fresh sardines, about 10–20 cm (4–8 inches), heads removed and gutted

100 g (3½ oz/¾ cup) pure sea salt, plus 2 teaspoons extra

1 teaspoon Ross's wholegrain mustard (page 248) or dijon mustard

2 teaspoons lemon juice

100 ml (3½ fl oz) extra virgin olive oil

Rinse the sardines in fresh water and pat dry with kitchen paper. Combine the salt and 500 ml (17 fl oz/2 cups) water in a bowl to make a brine. Place the sardines in the brine and leave for 1 hour — this will help firm up the flesh and draw out the blood and the strong fishy flavour.

Drain well, discarding the brine, and blanch the sardines in boiling water for 2 minutes, then immediately plunge into cold water. Drain, then pack the sardines into sterilised glass jars (see page 4) and set aside.

In a bowl, mix together the mustard, extra salt, lemon juice and olive oil and pour over the sardines, being sure to leave some air at the top of each jar for the ingredients to expand when you boil them. Seal the jars with tight-fitting lids.

Lay a tea towel (dish towel) in the base of a stockpot or large saucepan — this will stop the jars from rattling in the pot. Place the jars in a single layer on the tea towel, then fill the pot with enough water to cover the jars by at least 2 cm (¾ inch). Bring to the boil, then reduce the heat and simmer for 3 hours. Remove from the heat, and when cool enough to handle, remove from the jars and set aside to cool.

Allow the sardines to sit for 1 week before eating them. They should last up to 3 months but must be refrigerated once opened.

BOTTARGA

Makes 5 pieces, about 45–60 g (1½–2 oz) each

Bottarga is salted, cured fish (usually mullet) roe originating from Sardinia and Sicily. It is traditionally sliced, grated or sprinkled on seafood pasta dishes. Make sure your roe is as fresh as possible and not damaged in any way. You may need to order the roe from your fishmonger in advance — ask them for roe which has not been frozen. This gear can be a bit whiffy while it is drying, so find a place where you are not going to offend anyone.

Soak the roe overnight in a solution of water and salt — use 2 teaspoons salt per 1 litre (35 fl oz/ 4 cups) water. Remove the roe and pat dry using kitchen paper; discard the soaking liquid.

Lay out fresh kitchen paper on a tray and liberally sprinkle with salt. Place the roe on top and cover with more salt. Place this in the refrigerator for 3–4 days — you will need to replace the kitchen paper daily, adding a fresh layer of salt each time. After this time the roe will have firmed up. Use a skewer to poke a hole in each roe and thread them onto the butcher's twine in a long loop. Hang the roe in a cool dry place, about 12°C (54°F) for 10–14 days (or longer, if desired).

Remove the roe from the twine, brush with a little olive oil, wrap in plastic wrap and refrigerate — it should last for up to 3 months. Bottarga is best served freshly sliced or grated onto steaming hot pasta tossed in a robust extra virgin olive oil with lemon zest and chopped parsley.

5 whole fish roe or egg sacs (small eggs are best), about 70–100 g (2½–3½ oz) each

pure sea salt

butcher's twine

olive oil

SALT COD

Makes about 650 g–1.3 kg (1 lb 7 oz–3 lb)

*Salt cod has been a big part of many cultures for centuries. It is still a staple in Spain,
Portugal and Italy. Dry salting fish removes the water from it and prevents it from spoilage.
The fish is also dried after it is cured, in the same way as curing pork for air-dried ham.
To use salt cod, it needs to be reconstituted. The texture of the flesh becomes denser and
the flavour is also more pronounced than fresh fish. In Australia, you can also use
blue-eye trevalla, mulloway, pink ling or silver warehou.*

1–2 kg (2 lb 4 oz–4 lb 8 oz)
thick piece of fresh skinless
cod fillets

500 g (1 lb 2 oz) pure sea salt

muslin (cheesecloth)

Wash the cod and pat dry with kitchen paper.
Don't worry too much about removing the bones.

Rub three-quarters of the salt all over
the cod, pressing it into the flesh so that it
adheres to the surface. Wrap the cod in muslin
and sprinkle the remaining salt on top and
underneath. Arrange a wire rack in a large tray
or baking dish to catch any liquid. Place the cod
on the rack and refrigerate for 48 hours.

Unwrap the cod and rinse well in cold
water, then pat dry. Re-wrap the fish in a single
layer of fresh muslin. Return to the rack and
refrigerate for a further 7 days to dry out. Make
sure there is adequate air circulating around
the fish. You can tell the salt cod is ready when it
is slightly opaque and stiff all the way through.
Salt cod can be wrapped and stored in a cool
place for up to 3 months before being used.

To serve, you need to get the salt out of
the fish and reconstitute it. Do this by taking
the desired amount of salt cod and washing
it. Place in a small plastic tub and cover with
fresh water. Allow to sit at room temperature
for 24 hours, changing the water several times
(at least three) during this period. The salt cod
can then be fried in butter, braised with red
capsicums (peppers), tomatoes and onions or
made into fish cakes.

SALT-CURED FISH

PISSALADIÈRE

Serves 6–8

When Ross was working and living in Nice, he ended up working as a chef on a charter boat in the south of France. The French crew insisted he learn to cook pissaladière, which is similar to pizza with a bit more dough. This version strikes the perfect balance of sweet caramelised onion and salty anchovies. Together they would all sit on the bow of the boat and eat it, washed down with lots of red wine.

To make the topping, heat the butter and olive oil in a heavy-based frying pan over low heat. Add the onions, garlic and thyme and cook for 1 hour, stirring frequently — you want the onions to be soft and slightly caramelised, but not brown in colour. Remove from the heat, season with sea salt and freshly ground black pepper, and set aside to cool.

Once the onions have been cooking for about 40 minutes start preparing the base. Put the yeast in a bowl with 185 ml (6 fl oz/¾ cup) tepid water and the sugar and stir to combine — set aside until the mixture starts to froth.

Put the flour and salt into a stainless steel bowl. Add the olive oil and the yeast mixture to the flour and knead until it forms a dough. Turn out onto a lightly floured work surface and continue to knead the dough for 5 minutes, then return to the cleaned bowl lightly greased with olive oil. Cover with a clean tea towel (dish towel) and set aside in a warm place for 30–60 minutes, or until the dough has doubled in size. »

DOUGH BASE

1 teaspoon dried yeast

a pinch of sugar

300 g (10½ oz) '00' flour

a pinch of salt

60 ml (2 fl oz/¼ cup) olive oil

TOPPING

30 g (1 oz) butter

80 ml (2½ fl oz/⅓ cup) olive oil, plus extra, for brushing

1.5 kg (3 lb 5 oz) brown onions, very thinly sliced

5 purple garlic cloves, crushed

3 fresh thyme sprigs

12 salt-cured anchovy fillets (page 184), cut in half

1 handful pitted black pickled olives (page 228)

» If you have a pizza stone, place it in the oven and preheat your oven to 220°C (425°F/Gas 7) — this will give you a crisper base. Knead the dough into a large rectangle and roll it out on a lightly floured work surface to make a 40 x 30 cm (16 x 12 inch) rectangle to fit a large shallow baking tray and press it into the base of the lightly greased tray.

Brush the top of the dough with a little extra olive oil and spread the onions in an even layer over the top. Arrange the salt-cured anchovies in a criss-cross pattern over the onions. Add the olives to the spaces between and season with sea salt and freshly ground black pepper. Set aside for 15 minutes to give the dough a chance to rise again just slightly, or it will shrink when you bake it.

Place the pissaladière in the oven on top of the pizza stone, if using, and cook for 15–20 minutes, or until lightly coloured. Serve hot, with good company and lots of red wine.

LINGUINE WITH BOTTARGA AND LEMON

Serves 4

Pasta makes the perfect stage for the briny flavour of cured fish roe, or bottarga. Bottarga can vary greatly in flavour so use as much or as little as you like. If the roe is firm enough use a coarse grater, otherwise thinly slice it with a sharp knife and stir it through the hot pasta. The fried breadcrumbs add a yummy crunchy texture to this dish.

Cook the pasta in a saucepan of salted boiling water for 8–10 minutes, or until al dente. Drain well and set aside.

While the pasta cooks, start the topping. Heat 80 ml (2½ fl oz/⅓ cup) of the olive oil in a large frying pan over medium–low heat. Add the breadcrumbs and garlic and cook until the breadcrumbs are golden. Remove from the heat and stir through the bottarga, then tip the hot pasta into the pan and toss to combine. Add the parsley and extra bottarga, to taste, and serve with the remaining oil drizzled over the top.

500 g (1 lb 2 oz) dried pasta (linguine or spaghetti is perfect)

125 ml (4 fl oz/½ cup) extra virgin olive oil

150 g (5½ oz/2½ cups) fresh breadcrumbs

1 purple garlic clove, crushed

2 tablespoons grated or thinly sliced bottarga, plus extra to serve (page 186)

1 handful fresh flat-leaf (Italian) parsley, chopped

BRANDADE

Makes 700 g (1 lb 9 oz)

Brandade is an emulsion of salt cod and olive oil bound together with bread. Having gone to the trouble of making salt cod and getting the salt into the fish to cure it, for this dish, you now have to get all the salt out of the cod. To do this, cut the salt cod into large pieces and soak in cold water for at least 24 hours — you will need to change the water every 6 hours or so. Taste the fish to check all of the salt has gone. Variations of brandade are found across the Mediterranean, including some regions where cooks use floury potatoes instead of bread.

---

500 g (1 lb 2 oz) salt cod
(page 187), soaked

juice of 2 lemons

2 fresh flat-leaf (Italian)
parsley sprigs

2 bay leaves

6 whole black peppercorns

1 small onion, sliced

2 thick slices white bread,
crusts removed

100 ml (3½ fl oz) full-cream
(whole) milk

2½ tablespoons pouring
(whipping) cream

2 garlic cloves, finely chopped

100 ml (3½ fl oz) olive oil

Drain the salt cod and place in a large saucepan with half of the lemon juice, the parsley, bay leaves, peppercorns, onion and enough water to cover. Bring to the boil, then reduce the heat to low and simmer, covered, for 15 minutes. Drain the cod, discarding the cooking liquid. Let the cod cool slightly, then break the flesh into flakes, discarding any skin or bones that you find.

Put the bread into a food processor, then pour in the milk and cream. Let it soak for 5 minutes, then add the flaked fish and garlic and process until well combined and smooth.

With the motor running, slowly add the olive oil in a thin, steady stream and process until well combined and smooth. Season with the remaining lemon juice and some sea salt (be careful with the salt as the fish will already taste a bit salty) and freshly ground black pepper. Serve with fresh crusty bread.

PICKLED FISH

It seems the strangest of things to pickle fish. Taking something so fleeting, so precious as fresh fish and adding relatively harsh flavours. And we wouldn't suggest for a minute that you do it with very expensive line-caught, ice-slurried, sashimi-grade kingfish that you buy at the market. But we would, for flavour and efficiency, highly recommend it for a time of glut.

Vinegared fish is well regarded in many countries. The sprightly acidity of the vinegar cuts the richness of oily fish and creates a dish from what would otherwise be a single ingredient. Think of rollmops as a case in point. With good rye, they become the meal. A little bit of fish goes a long way.

Tuna preserved in a jar isn't true pickled seafood. You could add lemon juice or vinegar and a bay leaf to the recipe, but we like the pure flavour, where raw tuna is transformed into something similar to tinned tuna, but with better texture and flavour. It's just as versatile and makes a lot. Which means a successful weekend fishing charter can be turned into a year's worth of fish meals for you and your mates.

ROLLMOPS

Makes 10

Traditionally made in Europe from herring, you can use mackerel or other small, oily fish for a similar result. The fish is first pickled and then rolled around an onion to make neat little hors d'oeuvres. Our recipe is a quick version that you cook rather than cure for days. You can use cured, pitted olives or pickled gherkins inside the rollmops, too.

Put all of the ingredients, except the herring fillets and toothpicks, into a large saucepan with 500 ml (17 fl oz/2 cups) water. Bring to the boil, then reduce the heat to low and simmer for 10 minutes. Remove the onions with a slotted spoon and allow to cool slightly.

When the onions are cool enough to handle, wrap each one inside a herring fillet. Secure each rollmop with a toothpick and return to the vinegar mixture in the pan. Bring back to the boil. Turn off and let the fish cool in the liquor. Serve cold.

Rollmops keep well for several days in the refrigerator if completely covered with vinegar.

10 very small pickling onions, peeled

10 allspice berries

10 whole black peppercorns

2 tablespoons salt

3 tablespoons sugar

500 ml (17 fl oz/2 cups) white wine vinegar

10 small herring or mackerel fillets or pieces, about 10 x 2 cm (4 x ¾ inches)

toothpicks, for fastening

SOUSED MUSSELS

Makes about 500–600 g (1 lb 2 oz–1 lb 5 oz)

Delicious as a snack (with cider or beer) soused mussels are a flavour-packed morsel. Use to dress up a seafood salad, on dark rye with harissa (page 249), or tossed through potatoes with paprika and roasted red capsicum (pepper).

2 kg (4 lb 8 oz) fresh mussels

250 ml (9 fl oz/1 cup) dry white wine

2 bay leaves

½ purple garlic bulb, cut in half to expose the cloves

2 fresh lemon slices

250–400 ml (9–14 fl oz) white wine vinegar

De-beard the mussels and discard any that do not close when tapped. Rinse and drain well.

Put 100 ml (3½ fl oz) of the wine and 100 ml (3½ fl oz) water in a large saucepan and bring to the boil. Add the bay leaves, garlic and lemon slices, then reduce the heat to low and simmer for 5 minutes. Toss in the mussels and cover the pan, then increase the heat and cook for 4–5 minutes, shaking the pan regularly until all the mussels steam open.

Remove the mussels from the pan, reserving the cooking liquor. When they are cool enough to handle, take the mussel meat from each shell and place into sterilised glass jars (see page 4).

Strain and cool the cooking liquor and pour over the mussels so they are about half covered with liquid. Add the remaining white wine and enough vinegar to top up each jar — at least one quarter of the liquid needs to be vinegar. Seal with tight-fitting lids and refrigerate for at least 1 week before using. The soused mussels can be stored in the refrigerator for up to 3 months.

PRESERVED TUNA

Makes about 6 kg (13 lb 8 oz)

We started preserving tuna when Nick and Ross went fishing and we had way more fish than we could eat in a week, let alone in one go. You do need the bones and/or head for both flavour and for the gelatine that breaks down into the broth. Albacore is an excellent tuna to use because it's more sustainably caught by commercial fishers than yellowfin and in particular southern bluefin tuna. Do a big batch to make it worth putting up with the awful smell.

Put the tuna into a stockpot or large saucepan and cover with fresh, clean seawater. Seawater is, on average, made up of 3.5 per cent salt. To make your own, for every 1 litre (35 fl oz/ 4 cups) of water, add 35 g (1¼ oz) salt.

Place the pot on a huge burner, preferably outside because of the smell. Put it on the highest flame possible, bring to the boil, then reduce the heat to low and simmer for 4 hours, or until the fish is well cooked.

Remove from the heat and cover the pot with a lid to avoid things flying or falling in. Allow to cool enough so you can dip your hands in. Remove the tuna meat gently from the pot and break up into large pieces, discarding the head, bones and skin. Place the tuna pieces into sterilised glass jars (see page 4). Top up each jar with olive oil to about 5 mm (¼ inch) below the top, shaking gently to remove any air bubbles. Seal each jar immediately, though not too tight.   »

15 kg (33 lb 12 oz) whole albacore tuna (head, bones, skin on), cut into large chunks

seawater or about 1 kg (2 lb 4 oz) pure sea salt

good-quality olive oil

» Lay a tea towel (dish towel) in the base of a stockpot or large saucepan — this will stop the jars from rattling in the pan. Place the jars in a single layer on the tea towel, adding another clean tea towel and another layer of jars — you will need two layers with this quantity. Fill the pot with enough fresh water to cover the jars by at least 2 cm (¾ inch). Bring to the boil, then reduce the heat and simmer steadily for at least 2 hours. Remove from the heat, and when the jars are cool enough to handle, remove them from the pot and set aside to cool.

Store in a cool, dark place for at least 1 month if you're patient, to allow the flavours to develop. The tuna should keep for up to 3 months or even longer.

Once open, store the preserved tuna in the refrigerator and consume within a few days. We strongly recommend you use the fish in cooked dishes, heating the fish to at least 80°C (175°F) before consuming to minimise the risk of botulism.

Use as you would tinned tuna — in pasta, over hot new potatoes or in salads and the like.

NOTE: *The oil will tend to expand a little during the boiling process, so don't put the lids on too tightly or fill the jars too full. That said, the lids do have to be tight enough for the oil not to escape.*

NICK'S PICKLED FISH

Makes 1 kg (2 lb 4 oz)

This is a brilliant way to store excess fish for a very different kind of meal. The vinegar acts to cut the richness of the fish and the onion alone is delicious served with slices of buttered rye bread. Add the fish and you'll be in heaven. We have had success in pickling lots of different types of fish, from oily mackerel to delicate white-fleshed flathead, so this recipe should work for just about any type of fish.

Place the fish chunks in a bowl and sprinkle with 3 teaspoons of the salt. Cover and refrigerate for about 2 hours.

Meanwhile, put the vinegar, remaining salt, brown sugar, the mustard, coriander and fennel seeds, peppercorns, garam masala, ginger and chilli into a large saucepan. Bring to the boil for 5 minutes, then remove from the heat. Add the onions to the vinegar solution and leave for 1 hour to infuse.

Remove the fish from the salt and pat with kitchen paper, removing as much salt as possible. Layer the fish and onion in sterilised glass jars (see page 4), adding 2 bay leaves per jar. Cover the fish with the vinegar mixture and seal the jars with tight-fitting lids. Leave for 1 week before using. Store for up to 3 months in a cool, dark place.

Once opened, the pickled fish can be stored in the refrigerator. These make a great lunch-on-the-run when eaten with good rye or pumpernickel bread. If you have the time to drink a glass of ale with them, we suggest you do.

- 1 kg (2 lb 4 oz) firm, white-fleshed fish, skinned, bones removed and cut into 2 cm (¾ inch) chunks
- 25 g (1 oz) sea salt
- 1 litre (35 fl oz/4 cups) white vinegar
- 60 g (2¼ oz/⅓ cup) soft brown sugar
- 1 teaspoon brown mustard seeds
- 1 teaspoon coriander seeds
- 1 teaspoon fennel seeds
- 1 teaspoon whole black peppercorns
- ½ teaspoon garam masala
- 2 cm (¾ inch) piece fresh ginger
- 2–3 small dried red chillies, roughly chopped
- 4 brown onions, thinly sliced
- 2 fresh bay leaves per medium-sized jar

PICKLED OCTOPUS

Makes about 300 g (10½ oz)

1 litre (35 fl oz/4 cups) white wine vinegar

1 celery stalk, cut into rough chunks

1 small brown onion, sliced

3–4 fresh flat-leaf (Italian) parsley sprigs

3 fresh bay leaves

1 kg (2 lb 4 oz) baby octopus, gutted and cleaned (see note)

1 tablespoon pure sea salt, plus 1–2 teaspoons extra

6 small dried red chillies

1 purple garlic bulb, unpeeled and broken into cloves

10 whole black peppercorns

Put 250 ml (9 fl oz/1 cup) of the vinegar into a large saucepan with the celery, onion, parsley, 1 of the bay leaves and 600 ml (21 fl oz) water. Bring to the boil, then reduce the heat and simmer for 5 minutes. Add the octopus and salt and simmer for about 15 minutes. Remove from the heat, drain the octopus, discarding the cooking liquid and vegetables, and set aside.

Meanwhile, put the remaining vinegar, bay leaves, chillies, garlic, peppercorns and extra salt in a saucepan and bring to the boil. Reduce the heat and simmer for 5 minutes.

Take the drained octopus and place into sterilised glass jars (see page 4), pressing down well. Fill each jar with the hot vinegar solution, leaving 5 mm (¼ inch) at the top, then divide the bay leaves, chillies, garlic cloves and peppercorns between each. Seal with tight-fitting lids and leave in a cool, dark place for at least 1 week before opening. Pickled octopus can be stored for up to 3 months and should be kept in the refrigerator after opening. It is fantastic with slices of steamed waxy potato, dusted with paprika and drizzled with extra virgin olive oil.

NOTE: *To clean the octopus, use a small knife to carefully cut between the head and tentacles, just below the eyes. Grasp the body and push the beak out and up through the centre of the tentacles with your finger. Cut the eyes from the head by slicing a small disc off with a sharp knife. Discard the eye section. To clean the head, carefully slit through one side, avoiding the ink sac and scrape out the gut. Rinse under running water to remove any grit.*

ROASTED VITELLO TONNATO

Serves 8

In this version of the Italian classic, we've roasted a veal loin to add some more character. Serve with boiled new potatoes, or soft bread as a starter or light meal.

1 kg (2 lb 4 oz) veal loin

6 salt-cured anchovies (page 184)

90 ml (3 fl oz) extra virgin olive oil

200 g (7 oz) preserved tuna in oil (pages 202–203)

2 free-range egg yolks

200 ml (7 fl oz) mild-flavoured oil, such as sunflower or peanut

1½ tablespoons lemon juice or white wine vinegar (page 246)

30 g (1 oz) salted capers, soaked in water for 30 minutes, then drained

fresh flat-leaf (Italian) parsley, roughly chopped

1 finely shaved baby fennel, cut across the grain, or use some roughly chopped fennel tops (optional)

Preheat the oven to 220°C (425°F/Gas 7). Trim the veal loin well and rub with freshly ground black pepper. Mash three of the anchovies with 1 tablespoon of the olive oil to make a thick paste. Rub this paste all over the loin.

Heat another 1 tablespoon of the oil in a heavy-based frying pan over high heat and sear the loin on all sides. Place into the oven (ideally in the same pan if it's ovenproof, but on a tray is fine), then reduce the temperature to 160°C (315°F/Gas 2–3) and roast for about 15 minutes, or until the meat is cooked to medium. Remove from the oven, let the meat rest under foil and leave to cool completely.

Drain the tuna, reserving the oil. In a food processor, blend the tuna, remaining anchovies and the egg yolks until smooth. With the motor running, add the sunflower oil and remaining olive oil in a thin stream until well incorporated. Add the reserved tuna oil and the lemon juice, also with the motor running. Taste for salt and pepper.

To serve, thinly slice the veal, smother with the sauce and scatter over the capers, parsley and fennel, if using.

VEGETABLES AND CONDIMENTS

VEGETABLES AND CONDIMENTS

IMAGINE A PLOUGHMAN'S WITHOUT A PICKLE OR A PICKLED ONION? IMAGINE PIZZA MINUS THE OLIVES OR SUSHI WITHOUT PICKLED GINGER?

It might be less sexy than a string of salami drying in your garage or a wad of homemade butter on your sourdough but the beauty and importance of preserved vegies should not be overlooked (and quite frankly, not much turns us on more than a pantry crammed with jars and bottles of home preserving!).

The whole reason for preserving anything (be it pickled, smoked, fermented or dried) is to ensure a supply of it for a time when it is out of season and unavailable. This is never more true than for vegetables, which can be growing in the garden one week and gone the next, but whose goodness can be preserved for enjoying at any time.

In recent years, preserving has become the new black. Good chefs are turning their backs on their chemistry sets in favour of preserving kits, but even though it might be hip, there are good reasons to preserve a surplus of vegetables or eggs and it is not just about watching your pennies. It's about appreciating the seasonality of good food and wanting to capture the essence of this in a jar or bottle. In our world of 'whatever-you-want-whenever-you-want-it' produce, which has often passed through more time zones than Dr Who, this has never been more important.

PICKLING

Like most things, preserved vegetables exist now not because we have to have them, but because we want them. Once a way of keeping the surfeit of one season's harvest for later months, now the reason we make and eat preserved vegetables is because they add variety to our meals. The fact they lie in wait in the pantry for a hungry ploughman or office worker to snaffle them up for a quick flavour hit with dinner is just a bonus. As with any preserving, cleanliness is paramount to ensure a safe, delicious, long-lasting end product. Detailed instructions for sterilising your cooking equipment, bottles, jars and lids can be found on page 4.

VEGETABLES

Nothing makes for a quick lunch, a pasta on the run, or even a sandwich filling like a few semi-dried tomatoes. Or a few olives. These are the kinds of things that can turn a modest meal into an expression of your own kitchen. The olives you cure yourself won't be like the ones you buy. In a good way. Even shop-bought tomatoes start to pack a punch once dehydrated a little and left to marinate with local garlic in good olive oil.

Preserving vegetables is also about alchemy — by taking something as banal as a cabbage or an onion and transforming it into a potent pot of sauerkraut or pickling it in a spice-laden cider you can continue to appreciate it for many months, not just days.

PRESERVED MUSHROOMS

Makes a 1 litre (35 fl oz) jar or 4 x 250 ml (9 fl oz) jars

This is the best way we have found to keep mushrooms. They don't lose their earthiness or great texture or the natural, flavoursome juice that comes out during braising. This is a good recipe to play around with to suit your own taste — by adding different herbs and spices you can change the outcome considerably.

Preheat the oven to 160°C (315°F/Gas 2–3). Arrange the mushrooms, flat side down, in a single layer on two roasting trays. Take the butter and break it up by hand, then scatter it around the mushrooms.

Put all of the remaining ingredients into a blender or food processor (you can use a mortar and pestle if you prefer) and pulse until the flavourings are well combined. Spoon evenly over the top of the mushrooms, then wrap the trays tightly with foil to prevent the steam coming out during cooking.

Cook the mushrooms in the oven for 2 hours. Remove from the oven and set aside to cool. When the mushrooms have cooled, transfer the caps to sterilised glass jars and cover with the cooking liquid before sealing.

Preserved mushrooms can be stored in the refrigerator for months as long as the juice covers them completely. Add a bit of oil to completely seal if necessary. You can add them to everyday cooking or serve them cold as part of an antipasto — we like them heated on toast with a poached egg.

1 kg (2 lb 4 oz) field mushrooms

200 g (7 oz) salted cultured butter, softened (pages 12–13)

200 ml (7 fl oz) olive oil

1 purple garlic bulb, cut in half

1 bunch fresh chives, snipped

1 bunch fresh parsley, use flat-leaf (Italian) or curly, roughly chopped stalks and all

½ bunch fresh sage, roughly chopped stalks and all

½ bunch fresh thyme, roughly chopped stalks and all

1 tablespoon pure sea salt

1 tablespoon freshly ground black pepper

PICKLED ONIONS

Makes a 2 litre (70 fl oz) jar or 4 x 500 ml (17 fl oz) jars

These are a must-have in any pantry — once you have made up a batch they will keep for months. They are great to crack open when the boys come around to watch the cricket with a few beers.

1.5 kg (3 lb 5 oz) pickling onions, peeled

100 g (3½ oz) pure sea salt

PICKLING JUICE

1.25 litres (44 fl oz/5 cups) cider vinegar

1 teaspoon juniper berries

3 purple garlic cloves

1 teaspoon whole black peppercorns

3 bay leaves

1 tablespoon soft brown sugar

Put the whole peeled onions into a clean plastic bucket or similar-sized container and add the salt and 1 litre (35 fl oz/4 cups) water, stirring to combine. Place a plate directly over the top to keep the onions submerged and leave overnight.

Remove the onions from the salted water and rinse them in fresh water, then place them into sterilised glass jars (see page 4).

Put the vinegar, juniper berries, garlic, peppercorns, bay leaves and sugar in a large saucepan and bring to the boil. As soon as it boils, remove from the heat and pour over the onions, being careful not to burn yourself, then seal each jar with a tight-fitting lid and set aside to cool.

The pickled onions need to sit for 1 month before consuming. Store for up to 6 months in the cupboard and keep them in the refrigerator after opening.

DILL PICKLES

Makes a 1 litre (35 fl oz) jar or 4 x 250 ml (9 fl oz) jars

The hardest thing about making dill pickles is finding the cucumbers. So the best way around that is to grow your own. Most garden centres will have at least one variety of pickling cucumber, although you can pickle any variety if you can't find the smaller ones.

30 pickling cucumbers

1 bunch fresh dill

5 purple garlic cloves, peeled

1 tablespoon black mustard seeds

BRINE

450 ml (16 fl oz) white wine vinegar (page 246)

75 g (2½ oz) pure sea salt

Place the brine ingredients in a saucepan with 1.5 litres (52 fl oz/6 cups) water and bring to the boil. Once the salt has dissolved, remove from the heat and allow to cool. Set aside.

Wash the cucumbers in fresh cold water and drain well. Divide a few sprigs of dill in the bottom of sterilised glass jars (see page 4). Pack the cucumbers into the jars, standing them upright lengthways as tightly as possible. Divide the garlic, mustard seeds and remaining dill between the jars and add another layer of cucumbers over the top if needed. Pour enough brine into each jar to fill it and seal with tight-fitting lids.

Lay a tea towel (dish towel) in the base of a stockpot or large saucepan — this will stop the jars from rattling in the pot. Place the jars in a single layer on the tea towel, then fill the pot with enough fresh water to cover the jars by at least 2 cm (¾ inch). Bring to the boil, then reduce the heat and simmer steadily for 20 minutes. Remove the pot from the heat, and when the jars are cool enough to handle, remove them from the pot and set aside to cool.

Store the dill pickles in a dark cupboard for at least 1 month before opening, then in the refrigerator once opened.

MELANZANE

Makes a 600 ml (21 fl oz) jar

There are many different ways to make this traditional pickled eggplant and any Italian will always tell you their method is the best. We have found this one works for us — you can make as little or as much as you like depending on the size of your jar.

2 eggplants (aubergines), trimmed and thinly sliced into rounds

50 g (1¾ oz) pure sea salt

500 ml (17 fl oz/2 cups) white wine vinegar (page 246)

3 purple garlic cloves, whole

1 bay leaf

1 teaspoon chopped fresh flat-leaf (Italian) parsley

1 teaspoon chopped fresh oregano

a pinch of dried chilli flakes (optional)

good-quality olive oil, for filling

Arrange the eggplant slices in a stainless steel colander inside a bowl to catch the juices. Sprinkle over the salt and then turn to make sure they are coated all over. Place a plate on top of the eggplant to weigh it down. Leave overnight.

Squeeze out the eggplant slices to remove any liquid. Put the vinegar and 500 ml (17 fl oz/ 2 cups) water in a large saucepan and bring to the boil. Blanch the eggplant, in batches, for about 3 minutes. Drain well and set aside.

Put the garlic, bay leaf, parsley, oregano and chilli flakes, if using, in a bowl. Start to layer the eggplant into a sterilised glass jar (see page 4), adding a sprinkling of mixed herbs between each layer until it is packed tightly into the jar. Top up with olive oil and seal with a tight-fitting lid.

Lay a tea towel (dish towel) in the base of a stockpot or large saucepan—this will stop the jar from rattling in the pan. Place the jar on the tea towel, then fill the pot with enough fresh water to cover the jar by at least 2 cm (¾ inch). Bring to the boil, then reduce the heat and simmer for 10 minutes. Remove the pot from the heat, and when the jar is cool enough to handle, remove it from the pot and set aside to cool.

Store the melanzane in a dark cupboard for at least 2 weeks before opening, then in the refrigerator once opened.

VEGETABLES

PICKLED GINGER

Makes a 600 ml (21 fl oz) jar

This is a must if you make sushi at home. It keeps for ages so you won't need to make it that often. For the best results, use the freshest ginger you can find, which will ensure that hallmark pink tinge.

Wash the ginger root and rub off as much of the skin as possible (the younger the ginger the easier the skin will peel off). Slice the ginger as thinly as possible and place into a stainless steel bowl. Add the salt, toss to coat and leave for 1 hour.

Pat the ginger dry with kitchen paper, place it in a sterilised glass jar (see page 4). Set aside.

Put the vinegar and sugar into a saucepan and bring to the boil. As soon as it boils, remove from the heat, pour over the ginger and allow to cool before sealing with a tight-fitting lid. Preserved ginger can be stored in the refrigerator for up to 2 months.

500 g (1 lb 2 oz) fresh young ginger

1 teaspoon pure sea salt

375 ml (13 fl oz/1½ cups) rice wine vinegar

125 g (4½ oz) caster (superfine) sugar

PRESERVED ARTICHOKES

Makes a 2 litre (70 fl oz) jar or 4 x 500 ml (17 fl oz) jars

For years Ross did not like artichokes but we now know it was because he didn't know how to cook them. Not only is this a great tasting method but you can also keep them for up to a year in the cupboard — it pays to date the jars as you make them. Ross likes them best served warm with pasta and fresh rocket, or just at room temperature with some homemade prosciutto (pages 78–79).

1 litre (35 fl oz/4 cups) white wine vinegar (page 246)

500 ml (17 fl oz/2 cups) white wine

1 teaspoon dried chilli flakes

100 g (3½ oz/¾ cup) pure sea salt

1 tablespoon whole cloves

1.5 kg (3 lb 5 oz) small artichokes

500 ml (17 fl oz/2 cups) olive oil

3 fresh rosemary sprigs, blanched

3 bay leaves

Put the vinegar, wine, chilli flakes, salt and whole cloves into a stockpot or large saucepan.

Top and tail the artichokes and peel around the sides removing the dark green leaves until you get to the younger leaves; make sure you remove the hairy choke. Place them immediately into the pot as you go to prevent them from discolouring.

When you have prepared all of the artichokes, place the pot over high heat and bring to the boil. Reduce the heat to low and simmer for 30–35 minutes — they are cooked when the tip of a sharp knife slides easily into the centre. Remove from the heat and allow the artichokes to cool in the liquid.

Use a slotted spoon to remove the artichokes from the liquid and place them into a stainless steel bowl. Add the olive oil, rosemary and bay leaves and mix well to coat. Pack the artichokes lightly into sterilised glass jars (see page 4), making sure there are no air holes and there is enough oil to keep them submerged. Seal the jars with tight-fitting lids and store in the cupboard for up to 1 year. Refrigerate after opening.

THREE-DAY PICKLED CABBAGE

Makes 1 kg (2 lb 4 oz)

This is like a quick version of sauerkraut, without being sour. The cabbage is pounded and it starts to ferment but hasn't gone very far before you start to eat it. Sauerkraut (opposite), on the other hand, may take a couple of months to cure properly.

2 kg (4 lb 8 oz) white cabbage
2 tablespoons pure sea salt

Slice the cabbage very thinly, then put it into a large bowl and sprinkle over the salt. Massage the salt in well and continue to work it until the cabbage releases its own juices. By some miracle, and your strenuous work, the cells of the cabbage soften and it goes from leaves that feel dry to a sloppy mess. What you want is to keep on working it until there's enough juice for the cabbage to be submerged in its own juices. Find a container with a wide lid (a sterilised bucket or similar is good), put the cabbage and juices in it, place a plate over the top, then weigh it down (tins of food or bottled water will do for this), so it's submerged in the liquid. Leave for 3 days, taking the weight off every night and stirring the cabbage so it's more exposed to the air and then putting the weight back on every morning. After 3 full days, the cabbage will have pickled and be ready to eat. Store in a sterilised glass jars (see page 4) in the refrigerator for up to 1 month. Use on sandwiches, in place of sauerkraut, with sausages or ham.

SAUERKRAUT

Makes 1 kg (2 lb 4 oz)

As the name suggests, sauerkraut is soured cabbage, which has been through a fermentation stage to change its sulphurous notes to make it into a more acidic and complex vegetable. Serve it with the world's best hot dog (see page 146), on a Reuben sandwich (see page 111) or as an accompaniment to any cured meat dish. You can substitute the seeds with 3 tablespoons fresh chopped dill fronds.

2 kg (4 lb 8 oz) white cabbage

2 tablespoons pure fine sea salt

1 tablespoon caraway seeds or dill seeds (optional)

Shred the cabbage as finely as you can. This step is not important for pickled cabbage (opposite) but it is for sauerkraut; a mandolin works best.

Put the cabbage and salt in a large bowl and use your hands to massage the salt into the cabbage to release the juice until there's enough juice to cover it. Transfer to a container with a wide lid (a sterilised bucket or similar is good). If you want to flavour the sauerkraut with caraway seeds or dill seeds, add them now. Place a plate on top and weigh it down to keep it submerged — it's important that the cabbage doesn't float. If need be, add a little brine solution at the ratio of 50 g (1¾ oz) salt for 1 litre (35 fl oz/4 cups) water.

Cover the container with a clean tea towel (dish towel) to keep things out (like vinegar fly), and place in a cool, dark place to ferment. It will take about 1 month at 15° (60°F), about 2 weeks at 20°C (68°F). At 25°C (77°F) it may go a little bit soft, so aim for cooler rather than warmer. At cellar temperature (12°C/54°F), it may take a couple of months to ferment. If there is a white scum forming on top, it could be a mould, so scoop this off and replace with more brine as needed. Taste to make sure it's good, then transfer to sterilised glass jars (see page 4) and store in the refrigerator or a cool pantry for up to 2 months.

PICKLED OLIVES

This method first appeared in Matthew's book The Real Food Companion, *but this volume wouldn't be the same without including it.*

Every Greek and Italian immigrant has their own way of pickling olives, but there are a couple of ways to get olives brined without using caustic soda. First, pick consistently coloured olives, and avoid any that are bruised or have marks. A good greengrocer will be able to get the right types for pickling for you. If you are using green olives, which are an unripe version of the black olive, hit them with a hammer to crack them or slit them with a knife (being crisper than black olives, the salt can penetrate more easily when the flesh is broken a little).

Place the whole black or slit green olives in a clean bucket of fresh water (or use a similar non-reactive container) and allow to soak. (Don't mix up the colours — each needs to cure in its own time.) Change the water every day until they start to lose their really horrid, metallic character. Some people like to use boiling water to speed up the process. As the olives soak they are fermenting (you may start to see some bubbles form in the water) and will leach out some chemicals, which makes them good to eat.

When ready to brine (your taste buds will tell you — it usually takes 1–2 weeks for them to lose most of their bitterness, though they still won't be delicious until brine-cured); drain the olives.

Take a separate clean bucket or similar non-reactive container and pour in enough water to completely cover the olives. Stir in enough salt so that a whole fresh egg floats readily on the surface — it's about 1 cup of salt for each 2.5 litres (87 fl oz/10 cups) water. Submerge the olives in this brine by placing a plate over the top and weighing it down (tins of food or a water bottle are good) and then cover the bucket (to keep out any greeblies or dirt).

Leave the olives to cure for about 2 months. A cool dark place is best, to avoid mould that could grow on the surface. This white scum that forms, if you see it, should be scooped off the top to avoid it tainting the brine. Taste the olives before using.

Olives can then be stored under oil, in a marinade or left in the brine until ready to use. Drain off the brine, rinse them, and then transfer to sterilised glass jars (see page 4). Top them up with oil (adding herbs if you like) or a brine solution made up of ½ cup salt to 10 cups water.

Always rinse the olives before eating, particularly if they're bought. If they're too salty, they can be soaked in water to reduce their intensity, though this may take a couple of days and as many changes of water.

PRESERVED ROAST TOMATOES

Makes 400 g (14 oz) drained preserved tomatoes

Choose tomatoes that are grown and ripened in dirt, that have never been refrigerated and are more fleshy than juicy, in other words, egg or roma-style tomatoes. We partially dry them, which means they don't keep as long, but aren't as hard or sharp as sun-dried tomatoes. If you get bored waiting for them to roast, pull them out earlier and use them quicker — more moisture means they'll ferment quicker and start to smell like tomato wine.

1 kg (2 lb 4 oz) roma tomatoes, halved lengthways

1 tablespoon pure coarse sea salt

2–3 teaspoons sugar

2 tablespoons red wine vinegar (page 246)

1 handful fresh oregano, leaves picked

4 purple garlic cloves, peeled and bruised

1 teaspoon finely grated orange zest

1 star anise

about 250 ml (9 fl oz/1 cup) extra virgin olive oil

Preheat the oven to 120°C (235°F/Gas ½). Arrange the tomatoes, cut side up, on a baking tray and sprinkle the salt and sugar evenly over the top. Roast the tomatoes for about 2 hours, or until they are starting to dry, reducing the oven temperature if need be — you want the tomato to retain some squidginess, without being wet. The tomatoes should be about one-quarter of their original size; try to avoid them getting too brown.

Sprinkle over the vinegar and oregano, and return to the oven for a further 30 minutes, or until the vinegar has dried off the outside. Place the tomatoes (leave any salt on the tray out) in a large sterilised glass jar (see page 4) with the garlic, orange zest and star anise. Press down gently and cover with enough olive oil to submerge, then allow to cool to room temperature. Seal the jar with a tight-fitting lid and refrigerate. They'll be perfect after 2 days, and should keep for up to 2 weeks if cooked properly. The preserving oil is excellent used in pasta, on bruschetta or in salads, too.

THE DEFINITIVE PLOUGHMAN'S

Serves 1

A real ploughman's lunch, unlike the one you're often served in a British pub these days, is a simple meal made from wonderful ingredients that live mostly in the pantry. It should be hearty enough to satisfy a ploughman, but you can make it dainty enough to please the squire.

PER PERSON

1 chunk of bread, cut from a cob loaf

2 slices classic smoked English-style leg ham (pages 74–75)

100 g (3½ oz) cheddar cheese

2 pickled onions (page 219)

1 pickled pub egg (or substitute a hard-boiled egg) (page 243)

dark pickle, such as Branston pickle

25 g (1 oz) cultured butter (pages 12–13)

Simply choose the best-quality ingredients and arrange them all on a big plate, preferably one that is made from chunky pottery or a rough-hewn piece of wood. Serve with cider or a dark ale.

BEEF TARTARE

Serves 4

Although it seems odd to have a dish of raw meat in a chapter of vegetables, this is a great way to show off some of your pickled vegies and also some of the condiments (see pages 240–249). It is Nick's favourite version, adapted from a recipe he tried and loved in Anthony Bourdain's Les Halles Cookbook. Although the eye fillet is often used for tartare because of its beautiful texture, it lacks flavour so use sirloin — it has the best combination of both flavour and texture. Try and get dry-aged (not vacuum-packed) grass-fed beef rather than beef which has been finished on grain.

Trim all the fat from the sirloin. Finely chop the steak and set aside.

Place the egg yolks in a large non-reactive bowl and add the mustard and anchovies. Mix well, then add the tomato and worcestershire sauces, season with freshly ground black pepper and mix well again. Slowly whisk in the oil, then add the brandy and mix again. Fold in the pickled onion, capers, dill pickles, and parsley.

Add the chopped meat to the bowl and mix well using a spoon or your hands. Divide the meat evenly among four chilled dinner plates and, using a ring mould or a spatula, form it into disc shapes. Serve immediately with toast on the side.

500 g (1 lb 2 oz) sirloin steak

2 free-range egg yolks

2 tablespoons Ross's wholegrain mustard (page 248)

4 salt-cured anchovy fillets, pounded with the back of a knife (page 184)

2 teaspoons Grandpa Steve's tomato sauce (ketchup) (page 242)

1 teaspoon worcestershire sauce

2 tablespoons extra virgin olive oil

1 tablespoon brandy

1 small pickled onion, finely chopped (page 219)

2 teaspoons salted capers, rinsed and drained

3 tablespoons dill pickles , finely chopped (page 220)

4 fresh flat-leaf (Italian) parsley sprigs, finely chopped

VEGETABLES AND CONDIMENTS

234

BRAISED LAMB NECKS WITH OLIVES AND ROSEMARY

Serves 6

The neck of a lamb has almost more flavour than any other cut. Lambs are non-stop grazers and the muscles that wrap around the neck work hard all day and need long, slow cooking to break down the sinew and fibres. Throwing olives in with your braised lamb adds a warm earthiness to the meal.

3 large lamb necks, split in half lengthways and sinew removed

2 tablespoons plain (all-purpose) flour

olive oil

1 onion, finely diced

1 celery stalk, finely diced

1 carrot, finely diced

90 g (3¼ oz/½ cup) olives (page 238)

2 large fresh rosemary sprigs

3 purple garlic cloves, smashed with back of a knife

400 ml (14 fl oz) red wine

1 litre (35 fl oz/4 cups) meat stock

Preheat the oven to 180°C (350°F/Gas 4). Wash the lamb necks well and remove any blood and bone fragments. Dry them and place them in a sealed plastic bag with the flour. Shake the bag to lightly coat the necks. Heat the oil in a cast-iron casserole dish over medium heat. Add the necks and turn to seal on all sides — bone side down to start, then continue turning until they are brown all over. Remove and set aside.

Add the onion, celery, carrot, olives, rosemary and garlic to the dish and sauté for 5 minutes. Return the lamb necks to the dish, add the wine and bring to the boil. Reduce the heat to low and simmer for 10 minutes, or until the wine has reduced by half. Add the stock, bring back to the boil, then remove the dish from the heat and cover with a lid. Transfer to the oven and cook for 3–4 hours, checking occasionally and turning the necks if they are getting dry on top. When the meat falls from the bone, remove from the oven and lift out the necks. Allow to cool a little, then remove the meat from the bones and set aside.

Skim the fat from the liquid in the dish and simmer for 10 minutes, or until it has thickened slightly and is rich in colour. Return the meat to the sauce and heat through. Serve over mashed potato or with couscous or lentils.

TAPENADE

Makes 250 g (9 oz)

The success of making a tapenade is totally reliant on good olives. It is a simple paste but it needs a good product to drive it. We recommend sourcing the best olives you can because you will get the best results. There are many variations of this recipe so you can play with the base one to get the result you want. This is also a handmade recipe, without the use of a food processor or blender, because we find it comes out a lot better with a little extra love.

First, pit all of the olives, then chop them and place them in a stainless steel bowl. Crush the garlic and roughly chop it with the anchovies and add them to the bowl. Roughly chop the capers with the parsley and add to the bowl, then add the lemon juice.

Stirring constantly with a wooden spoon, slowly add the olive oil until well combined; season with freshly ground black pepper. Store the tapenade in a sterilised glass jar (see page 4) in the refrigerator for up to 3 months — it is great served with fish and fresh bread

- 200 g (7 oz) good-quality black olives (page 228)
- 1 purple garlic clove, peeled
- 3 salt-cured anchovy fillets (page 184)
- 1 tablespoon baby salted capers, rinsed and squeezed dry
- 1 tablespoon chopped fresh flat-leaf (Italian) parsley
- juice of 1 lemon
- 1½ tablespoons extra virgin olive oil

CONDIMENTS

What would a hot dog be without mustard? A barbecue without tomato sauce? Imagine what life would be like without mayonnaise or vinegar. Imagine a life less lived. Condiments can take an average meal and make it transcend great heights. They're designed to be flavoursome, enriching every dish you put them with. They're also a great place to start your own mini-deli — because the recipes aren't too complicated, you don't need fancy equipment, and often the results can be tried relatively soon after you've made them.

241

GRANDPA STEVE'S TOMATO SAUCE

Makes about 6 litres (210 fl oz)

Celebrating Australia's love of rhyming slang, in Nick's family this sauce is only ever known as 'dead horse'. Nick inherited his grandparents handwritten cookbook and in it was this recipe, dated 1933 and written in neat copperplate. The original recipe was written in pounds and ounces and was just a list of ingredients and quantities, without a method. The Cornish pasties Steve made were also legendary, but really they were just a vehicle for his 'dead horse'.

Put the vinegar, sugar, salt, garlic, allspice, cloves and cayenne pepper into a heavy-based saucepan and bring to the boil. Add the tomato, onion and apple, reduce the heat to low and simmer, uncovered, for 2 hours, stirring frequently until the mixture has thickened and the tomatoes have broken down. Remove from the heat and allow to cool slightly before transferring to a food processor or blender and process until smooth (or you can push it through a sieve or a mouli to get a similar result).

Return the sauce to a clean pan and bring back to the boil. Remove the pan from the heat and pour the sauce into sterilised glass jars or bottles (see page 4). Seal immediately with tight-fitting lids. This sauce will keep for up to 12 months, which means you'll be ready to make it again in time for the next tomato season.

You can serve the sauce with just about anything — it's great with snags and eggs, but we also like it on top of grilled cheese on toast.

1 litre (35 fl oz/4 cups) white vinegar

1 kg (2 lb 4 oz/4½ cups) white sugar

200 g (7 oz) pure sea salt

6 purple garlic cloves, chopped

30 g (1 oz) ground allspice

15 g (½ oz) ground cloves

1 teaspoon cayenne pepper

5 kg (11 lb 4 oz) tomatoes, peeled and chopped

1 kg (2 lb 4 oz) brown onions, chopped

1 kg (2 lb 4 oz) green cooking apples, peeled, cored and chopped

PICKLED PUB EGGS

Makes 12

Nothing makes you want to order your second pint faster than a pickled egg, pulled from a big jar on the bar! With pub eggs in the fridge and home brew in the cellar, the temptation is even greater.

500 ml (17 fl oz/2 cups) cider or white wine vinegar (page 246)

1 brown onion, sliced and separated into rings

2 purple garlic cloves

2 teaspoons soft brown sugar

¼ teaspoon dried chilli flakes

2 whole cloves

20 whole black peppercorns

⅛ teaspoon fennel seeds

¼ teaspoon yellow mustard seeds

1 fresh bay leaf

1 teaspoon salt

12 hard-boiled free-range eggs, peeled and cooled

Put the vinegar, onion, garlic, sugar, spices, bay leaf and salt into a saucepan with 185 ml (6 fl oz/¾ cup) water. Bring to the boil and boil for 5 minutes — careful not to inhale it!

Pack the eggs loosely into a wide-mouthed sterilised glass jar (see page 4) and pour over the hot vinegar mixture. Cool to room temperature, cover and leave for 1 week in the refrigerator to complete the pickling process before eating. They can be stored for up to 6 weeks.

CONDIMENTS

VINEGAR

Makes about 1.25 litres (44 fl oz/5 cups)

Making vinegar is relatively simple in theory — we've all made it accidentally by leaving an open bottle of wine on the bench for a couple of weeks. To do it in a controlled way, you need to get a live mother, the cloudy, thick liquid that forms in the bottom of opened vinegar, to break down wine (or other alcohol) into vinegar. This takes time and not much else. We tend to use bits of leftover high-alcohol wines to start the vinegar and add to it over a couple of weeks as we have more. Good wine makes good vinegar, but is less likely to be kicking around as dregs in the bottom of the bottle. Hiccup.

Fill a 2 litre (70 fl oz) capacity wide-mouthed non-reactive container with the wine and the mother. Slosh it around and leave it somewhere that's about 20°C (68°F) and stable in temperature. Cooler is fine, but it will just take longer to react. At some point the famed vinegar fly will start to hang around, probably within hours, so cover the container with the muslin.

Take the muslin off for a half hour or so every day, if you think of it, to let the wine really breathe. Don't worry if you forget. The alcohol in the wine will gradually change to acetic acid, the flavour and sharpness we associate with vinegar. This will take roughly 2 weeks, but it does depend on the mother, the temperature and the amount of air that the wine is exposed to. Taste every day after the first week, and when it seems to be appropriately sharp, transfer to smaller, sterilised glass bottles (see page 4) — avoiding the mother if it's large and snotty — and keep in the refrigerator. If the bottles are airtight, the vinegar could be stored in the pantry until opened. Once opened, store in the refrigerator as the vinegar keeps breaking down and will eventually lose its acidity otherwise.

- **1.5 litres (52 fl oz/6 cups) wine, red or white, or perhaps a mix of both**
- **100 ml (3½ fl oz) mother from another wine vinegar, if you can get one (use a vinegar that hasn't been pasteurised, the sort you need to keep in the fridge)**
- **muslin (cheesecloth) or similar, for covering**

VEGETABLES AND CONDIMENTS

246

ROSS'S WHOLEGRAIN MUSTARD

Makes 250 g (9 oz/1 cup)

Mustard is a must in everyone's cupboard. This recipe is for wholegrain mustard but you can simply add all of the mustard seeds before blending to make a smoother version.

Place the black and yellow mustard seeds in a non-reactive bowl with the vinegar. Stir to combine, cover, and leave overnight.

Put two-thirds of the seeds and all the liquid into a food processor or blender, add the salt and lemon juice and process to make a smooth paste.

Transfer to a stainless steel bowl and stir in the remaining mustard seeds until combined.

Spoon the mustard into a sterilised glass jar (see page 4) and seal with a tight-fitting lid. Leave in the cupboard for 1 month before you use it. After you open it keep the mustard refrigerated — it will last for up to 6 months.

40 g (1½ oz) black mustard seeds

60 g (2¼ oz) yellow mustard seeds

125 ml (4 fl oz/½ cup) white wine vinegar (page 246)

1 teaspoon pure sea salt

juice of 1 lemon

HARISSA

Makes 300 g (10½ oz)

When Ross was working as a chef in London he first experienced cooking with north African cuisine, due to the fact that most of the kitchen porters in the restaurant were Algerian. He would often ask them to cook for the staff or help create specials, which they would proudly do. This harissa recipe is the one they showed him — it is fantastic served with fish or any type of fowl or game bird.

10–15 large dried red chillies

1 red capsicum (pepper), halved and seeded

2 purple garlic cloves

½ teaspoon pure sea salt

1 teaspoon ground cumin

1 teaspoon ground coriander

½ teaspoon ground caraway seeds

60 ml (2 fl oz/¼ cup) olive oil

juice of 1 lemon

Soak the dried chillies in a bowl of hot water for 5 minutes.

Preheat the oven to 200°C (400°F/Gas 6). Rub the outside of the capsicum with a touch of olive oil, place on a roasting tray and cook in the oven for 10 minutes, or until the skin has blackened and started to blister. Remove from the oven and when cool enough to handle, peel off the skin, roughly chop the flesh and place in a food processor or blender.

Remove the chillies from the bowl, then cut them in half lengthways, remove and discard any seeds and squeeze out any excess water. Place in the food processor with the remaining ingredients and process to a fine paste.

Spoon the harissa into a sterilised glass jar (see page 4) and keep refrigerated. It will keep for up to 1 month.

WARM POTATO SALAD WITH MUSTARD CRÈME FRAÎCHE

Serves 6

1 kg (2 lb 4 oz) waxy potatoes, such as pink-eye or kipfler

2–3 tablespoons Ross's wholegrain mustard (page 248)

150 g (5½ oz) crème fraîche (page 9)

2 teaspoons lemon juice

50 g (1¾ oz) dill pickles (page 220), roughly chopped

2–3 tablespoons fresh dill, chopped

Scrub the potatoes well and cut into evenly sized chunks if they are large. Place in a large saucepan with enough cold salted water to cover. Bring to the boil, then reduce the heat to low and simmer until tender — you should be able to easily pierce through to the centre with a knife.

While the spuds cook, mix together the mustard, crème fraîche and lemon juice in a bowl until combined.

When the potatoes are cooked, drain them and immediately toss with the crème fraîche mixture, the dill pickles and the dill. Serve with pastrami (see page 107), some smoked trout (see page 174) or as part of a barbecue meal. The salad would nearly become an entire meal in itself if you added chunks of grilled frankfurter (see page 140) to it.

BARBECUED HARISSA QUAIL WITH TABOULEH

Serves 4

You can buy quails that have already been butterflied (boned) but if you can't get these then you will need to 'spatchcock' the quails. In Australia we seem to think that spatchcock is a small chicken (properly known as a poussin). Spatchcock is the cut of a bird that is split down the backbone and flattened out, leaving the bones in.

Place the birds in a stainless steel bowl and rub the harissa all over to coat. Cover and refrigerate until needed.

To make the tabouleh, chop the tomatoes and drain the juice by placing in a sieve over a bowl. Set aside. Rinse the burghul well, then drain and tip into a separate stainless steel bowl. Cover with boiling water and leave to soak for 25 minutes. Drain well, then pat the burghul dry using a clean tea towel (dish towel). Place on a large serving platter. Add the drained tomato, the parsley, spring onion, mint, lemon juice and olive oil and mix well; season with sea salt and pepper. Cover with plastic wrap and set aside until you are ready to serve — tabouleh is best eaten at room temperature.

Light your barbecue chargrill — if you have a wood-fuelled barbecue, the quail will have a better taste. (You can also cook the quail in a large heavy-based frying pan.) Once it is hot, place the bird, breast side down, to begin. Cook the quails for about 15 minutes in total, turning every 3 minutes or so to prevent the marinade from burning. The quail will also taste better if you let them rest in a warm place, off the heat, for at least 5 minutes. Serve the quail over the tabouleh on the platter so the flavour from the birds runs into the salad.

4 whole quails, spatchcocked

80 g (2¾ oz/⅓ cup) harissa (page 249)

TABOULEH

4 tomatoes

75 g (2½ oz) burghul (bulgur)

1 bunch fresh flat-leaf (Italian) parsley, coarsely chopped including the stalks

6 spring onions (scallions), chopped

1 small handful fresh mint, chopped

juice of 1 lemon

2 tablespoons extra virgin olive oil

VEGETABLES AND CONDIMENTS

HORSERADISH AND MUSTARD MAYONNAISE

Makes 350 g (12 oz)

This is a pungent mayonnaise that is perfect for dolloping on corned beef, ham or eggs. The horseradish makes it a good seafood accompaniment, too.

Put a clean tea towel (dish towel) or place a rubber mat over the top of a saucepan and place a large bowl over that (this stabilises the bowl and prevents the bowl from spinning as you whisk). Put the egg yolks, mustard, horseradish and vinegar in the bowl, whisk to combine, then slowly pour in both of the oils in a thin steady stream, whisking the whole time.

Adjust the taste with salt, freshly ground black pepper and the lemon juice. You can use the mayonnaise immediately, but if you're using fresh horseradish, it's best to pop it into the refrigerator for a few hours to let the flavours settle. Transfer to a sterilised glass jar (see page 4), seal with a tight-fitting lid and refrigerate for up to 1 week.

2 free-range egg yolks

1–2 teaspoons Ross's wholegrain mustard (page 248)

1 teaspoon grated fresh horseradish or horseradish cream

2 teaspoons white wine vinegar (page 246)

200 ml (7 fl oz) vegetable oil

2½ tablespoons extra virgin olive oil

1–2 teaspoons lemon juice

MATTHEW'S VINAIGRETTE DRESSING

Makes about 150 ml (5 fl oz)

You can adjust the basic vinaigrette with herbs to suit your tastes, garden, or end use. This vinaigrette can be used on the warm potato salad, with a smoked tuna, potato and olive salad (see page 180), over steamed green beans or asparagus, drizzled over sliced tomatoes or with a carpaccio or similar. It is great as a dip for boiled globe artichokes or to drizzle over bresaola (see page 106). You can even use it on lettuce leaves — shock, horror!

2 teaspoons dijon mustard

2 tablespoons extra virgin olive oil

80 ml (2½ fl oz/⅓ cup) red wine vinegar (page 246), or less, to taste

2 teaspoons fresh oregano (or basil), chopped

2 teaspoons fresh chervil, chopped (optional)

1 teaspoon fresh flat-leaf (Italian) parsley, chopped (optional)

1–2 purple garlic cloves, crushed

a pinch of sugar

In a bowl, whisk together the mustard, olive oil, vinegar, herbs, garlic and sugar. Taste for acidity, and season with sea salt and freshly ground black pepper. This vinaigrette will keep in the refrigerator for up to 1 week.

INDEX

INDEX

ACKNOWLEDGEMENTS

While our names appear on the cover, this book, as usual, is a result of team effort. We'd like to give our sincere gratitude to our editors Sonia Grieg and Jacqueline Blanchard for wrangling three different styles and very complex recipes into a glorious tome. Thanks to the team at Murdoch Books, especially Sally Webb, our publisher, and Tania Gomes for yet another gorgeous design. Thank you to our wonderful helpers in the kitchen Jo Cook and Michelle Crawford, stylist Charlotte Bell, producer of the telly show Sonja Armstrong and the team at Essential Media, and most of all to all those generations of great preservers and cooks who came before. We also feel blessed to have had photographer Alan Benson on board, whose yummy shots leap off the page.

Matthew would like to thank Sadie for her grace and charm in the face of the usual photographic onslaught, the team at SBS, including Erik Dwyer, who continue to put their faith in a show about a goose from the city trying to grow geese (and other things) in the country, and to Ross and Nick — mates, business partners and fellow flavour chasers who continue to inspire and amaze.

Ross would like to thank his wife Emma and son Felix for being there for him, as well as family and friends that have helped him along the way, and Matthew and Nick for bullying him into yet another venture. A special thanks goes to Sadie for making this book possible.

Nick wishes to thank, above all, the incredible LJ, who fills all the gaps he leaves in their lives and lets him pursue his dreams at the expense of his own. To his amazing girl Tilla and awesome boy Wilkie – 'love ya'. Big thanks to all the people that give him the freedom to do the things he wants to do rather than the things he ought to be doing: Anne Dechaineux, the crew at Bruny Island Cheese Co and Spanky at A Common Ground, to name a few. He would also like to thank Sadie Chrestman, who has the uncanny knack of being able to distinguish between his good ideas and those which are 'just another of Nick's enthusiasms'. Lastly, Matthew and Ross ... thanks, not just for this book, but also for constantly bringing value, humour, purpose, adventure, mateship and great food into his life.

Published in 2012 by Murdoch Books Pty Limited

Murdoch Books Australia
Pier 8/9
23 Hickson Road
Millers Point NSW 2000
Phone: +61 (0) 2 8220 2000
Fax: +61 (0) 2 8220 2558
www.murdochbooks.com.au
info@murdochbooks.com.au

Murdoch Books UK Limited
Erico House, 6th Floor
93–99 Upper Richmond Road
Putney, London SW15 2TG
Phone: +44 (0) 20 8785 5995
Fax: +44 (0) 20 8785 5985
www.murdochbooks.co.uk
info@murdochbooks.co.uk

For Corporate Orders & Custom Publishing contact Noel Hammond,
National Business Development Manager, Murdoch Books Australia.

Publisher: Sally Webb
Designer: Tania Gomes
Photographer: Alan Benson
Stylist: Charlotte Bell
Editor: Jacqueline Blanchard
Food Editor: Sonia Greig
Home Economists: Nonie Dwyer, Michelle Crawford, Jo Cook
Project Manager: Livia Caiazzo
Production Controller: Joan Beal

A cataloguing-in-publication entry is available from the catalogue
of the National Library of Australia at www.nla.gov.au.

A catalogue record for this book is available from the British Library.

Printed by 1010 Printing International Limited, China

IMPORTANT: Those who might be at risk from the effects of salmonella poisoning (the
elderly, pregnant women, young children and those suffering from immune deficiency
diseases) should consult their doctor with any concerns about eating raw eggs.

OVEN GUIDE: You may find cooking times vary depending on the oven you are using.
For fan-forced ovens, as a general rule, set the oven temperature to 20°C (35°F) lower
than indicated in the recipe.

We have used 20 ml (4 teaspoon) tablespoon measures. If you are using a 15 ml
(3 teaspoon) tablespoon add an extra teaspoon of the ingredient for each tablespoons